HEATHER McKAY'S
COMPLETE BOOK OF SQUASH

HEATHER McKAY'S

COMPLETE BOOK
OF SQUASH

by Heather McKay
with Jack Batten

BALLANTINE BOOKS · NEW YORK

Library of Congress Cataloging in Publication Data

McKay, Heather
   Heather McKay's Complete book of squash.

   1. Squash rackets (Game)   I. Batten, Jack, joint author.   II. Title.
III. Title: Complete book of squash.
GV1004.M32 1979   796.34′3   78-27080
ISBN 0-345-28271-X
ISBN 0-345-28250-7 pbk.

This edition published by arrangement with Macmillan of Canada

Published simultaneously in hardcover and trade paperback.

Manufactured in the United States of America

First Ballantine Books Edition: March 1979

1 2 3 4 5 6 7 8 9 10

Photographs by Terry Hancey

Grateful acknowledgements to:
International Squash Rackets Federation for 'Playing Rules for International Game' and Definitions of Terms; United States' Squash Rackets Association for 'North American Rules'; compiled by the Canadian Squash Racquets Association. Reprinted with permission from Squash Ontario.

Contents

An Introduction to Heather McKay by Jack Batten

"Let's have a bit of a hit," Heather McKay said to me, and — oh, *fool!* — I accepted with enthusiasm. It's one thing to watch the world's most accomplished woman squash player from the safety of a gallery. It's another and more treacherous matter to step onto a court with her. I took the step, and over the dread few minutes that followed, I found myself dazzled, bewildered, helpless, and ultimately routed.

I'm a squash player of unbounded eagerness but easily circumscribed talent, a plugger who rightly belongs in the D class at the Toronto Squash Club, where Heather and her husband Brian reign as the resident professionals. In one way, my limitations made me a perfect foil for Heather. I was in the same position of awed admiration as, say, an engineering student watching an astronaut pilot a rocket to the moon. Heather was so far beyond my prayers and possibilities as a squash player that I qualified as an ideal bystander to chronicle her magnificent gifts.

Moving on the court beside her — we're the same height, five feet six, and she outweighs me by about ten pounds, 135 to 125 — I was immediately aware of her compact power. Her right arm and thighs radiated strength, and when she stroked the ball, always with a motion that was deceptive in its grace and ease, it rocketed off the front wall of the court with a directness, purpose and consistency that were uncanny. Heather toyed with her repertoire of shots. She hit tricky boasts from the back corners of the court, banged volleys on lines as straight as a string, sent up teasing lobs, drove effortlessly for length. There was an immaculate quality about her play, as she converted squash for those few minutes into a game from a textbook. It was sport turned to art. It was bewitching. And for me, rooted helplessly on the court, it was a trifle embarrassing.

At least, I thought, I share the humiliation with the world's best women squash players (and not a few of the top men) of the past couple of decades. Heather has beaten all of them, sometimes in devastingly swift order. She took a crushingly brief fourteen minutes to dispose of the excellent Anna Craven Smith of England in the finals in the 1965 British Championships. Indeed, in five matches through the entire tournament that year, Heather needed to linger on court for a mere sixty-five minutes. Victory has been a habit with her. Beginning in 1962, she won sixteen consecutive British Championships, and beginning in 1960 she won fourteen consecutive Australian Championships. She took the one and only Women's World Open Championship, held in Australia in 1976, along with a couple of hundred other lesser tournaments. In her lifetime of competition, Heather has lost so few matches — just two, a quarter-final of the 1960 New South Wales Championship and the finals of the 1962 Scottish Championship — that her setbacks are measured only in the *games,* not the matches, other women have managed to sneak from under her nose. Have there been many of them? Hardly a handful. Only ten women have won tournament games against Heather, the most recent occurring in the semifinals of the 1977 British Open when Sue Cogswell of England took the third game after Heather had won the first two. Cogswell's victory was a case of not letting sleeping dogs lie because in the fourth game an aroused Heather despatched Cogswell in a crisp 9-0. Heather doesn't tolerate defeat. She doesn't need to. Her list of triumphs is limitless and unparalleled. "Heather McKay's record," *Sports Illustrated* summed up in early 1977, "is unmatched by any woman in any sport."

The story of Heather's march to dominance reaches back for its beginnings to the years of World War II when she grew up in a small Australian town in the state of New South Wales called Queanbeyan. Many of the eleven thousand citizens who lived there when Heather was young worked as civil servants in the country's capital, Canberra, seven miles away. There was farming in the nearby countryside, some logging, and Queanbeyan itself later boasted a bottling plant for Coca Cola. Frank Blundell, Heather's father, worked at Morton's Bakery, baking bread on a shift that kept him at the job from ten at night till five in the morning. For much of the rest of the day, he devoted himself to the large family that he and his wife, the former Dulcie Neale, were raising. There were six boys and five girls. Number eight on the list, born July 31, 1941, was the child destined to make Queanbeyan famous: Heather Pamela Blundell.

Frank Blundell loved sports. Through the 1920s and '30s, he was one of the best rugby league footballers that New South Wales ever produced, and when he retired from football in 1938, he busied himself with tennis. He made certain that all of his children took their turns in sports, at least a couple at a time. "Every one of us," Heather remembers, "played lots of games." Tennis came first for Heather when she was ten, then field hockey at thirteen. She won praise and prizes in both. In her late teens, she discovered squash.

By this time, she had finished school and was working as a clerk selling papers and cards and pencils in Mr. Gray's news agency on Monaro Street in Queanbeyan. "It was a friendly job," she says. "I mean, I knew almost everybody in town by sight anyway." One man she knew by sight was Leo Casey, the partner in a local car agency. Leo Casey, now deceased, changed Heather's life because it was he who, as a sort of publicity move for the car agency, installed something at his place of business that was new to Queanbeyan, two squash courts.

It was 1959, and the squash boom was just getting under way in Australia. The country had already asserted itself in other sports with international triumphs. At the 1956 Olympic Games, it had won fourteen gold medals, and in the years immediately after World War I, it had brought home and kept home eleven Davis Cups. John Landy ran two sub-four-minute miles in the space of a single week, and Dawn Fraser emerged as perhaps the world's most remarkable woman swimmer. With all these successes in hand, Australians decided it was time to get serious about squash. An English men's touring squash team had visited Australia in the late 1950s and thrashed the locals. That ignominy set off a squash mania that reached into Queanbeyan and Leo Casey's car agency.

At first, eighteen-year-old Heather and her friends looked on the courts as a place to keep their legs in shape for field hockey, which ranked as their number one sport. "Hell, we were just out there hitting and running," Heather recalls. But she could hit and run better than anyone else, and during Easter week of 1960, she was persuaded to travel down the road to Woollongong and enter the New South Wales Country Championships. To the surprise of one and all, she won the Country Junior Championship and the Country Women's Championship. In June, she went to Sydney for the New South Wales Open Championships. She won the junior, and in the women's tournament she lost to the eventual champion, Yvonne West, in the quarter finals, one of the two smudges on her otherwise perfect lifetime record.

"I might have won," Heather says. "I was two games up on Yvonne and leading her 8-2 in the third, and then I got pooped. I'd already played a hard junior match that day, and I didn't have any energy left. But I went home happy. I hadn't expected to do anything in the tournaments at all."

Her performance earned Heather a position on the New South Wales team to play in the Australian Championships in Brisbane in August, and the squash world began its long acquaintance with Heather McKay. Within twelve months after she'd taken up the game, against all odds and against the cream of the country's female squash players, Heather won the Australian Championships. "That was a bloody shock to everybody," Heather puts it succinctly. "No one had ever heard of me, and there I was winning the whole thing." From that win, Heather went into a perpetual orbit of victory. Once launched, she couldn't be stopped. With the exception of the loss in the 1962 Scottish Championship during her first trip outside of Australia, she simply kept on winning. She won at home and she won abroad. She won with her extraordinary physical fitness and her impeccable racket finesse. She won on instinct and she won with intelligence. She was the best in the world.

Through the 1960s and '70s, Australia and the rest of the squash countries continued to acknowledge Heather's greatness. In 1967, she was named Australia's Sportsman of the Year, a much valued honor in that country, succeeding the impressive likes of Herb Elliott and Ron Clarke from track, Lionel Rose from boxing and a lengthy list of tennis stars. On January 1, 1969, she was made a Member of the British Empire "for services in sporting and international spheres," and in 1973 the Helms Athletic Foundation of California put her in its Hall of Fame, the first squash player to be admitted. The readers of the *Sunday Mail* of Australia had their say in February 1975 when they voted on the country's number one sports representative of the previous twenty years. Heather finished first, ahead of, in order, Dawn Fraser, Rod Laver, Margaret Court and Herb Elliott.

But in a curious way, for all the honors, she remained one of the world's least known great athletes. Certainly she didn't prosper financially; Heather was an amateur and she had to earn her keep. For nine years, she worked as a receptionist at the Bellevue Hill Squash Club in Sydney, and along the way, to help finance her forays to far-off tournaments, she moonlighted at a bizarre variety of part-time jobs, even serving a stint in the early 1970s as a taxi despatcher. Can anyone imagine Chris Evert at the peak of her championship powers sitting in front of a microphone ordering up cabs?

Bellevue Hill brought her one enduring benefit, an introduction to a husky, handsome, young Sydney bloke named Brian McKay. Brian's trade was as a fitter and turner, working with lathes, but he was also a splendid athlete. He played football and water polo, and in the early 1960s he became one of the new generation of Australia's squash pros, teaching and coaching in the evenings and on weekends. Heather and Brian, in love with one another and with squash, made an ideal match, and on December 13, 1965, they were married. By the late 1960s, they began working as a team in squash clubs,

Heather the amateur managing and Brian the pro teaching. They ran clubs in Brisbane and Canberra, and in June 1975, a year after Heather had also turned professional, they moved to the Toronto Squash Club in the city that, more than any other in North America, had blossomed through the 1970s as a new squash capital. Heather and Brian settled into a flat in the Beaches section of Toronto, close by a boardwalk along Lake Ontario where they established themselves as regular early-morning joggers.

To know Heather — to work with her on a book like this one, as I have — is to become her devoted fan, as I have. She's a woman without pretence or airs. Behind her small remaining shield of small-town shyness, she seems forever ready to accept friends and strangers on whatever terms they offer. Heather has no notions of showing the world anything except honesty and a smile, and she trusts the world to respond in kind. She is pretty and she's feminine. She has a trim figure and a small, clearly defined face. A reporter from *The Scotsman* of Edinburgh, writing in January 1962, took admiring note of her "elfin-like features," and the description is still true in the late 1970s. Her hair is dark brown and cut close to her head like a natural cap. Her eyes are large and brown, her voice is direct, and she likes to laugh.

She's Australian in her affection for a good chat, and she's Australian in her choice of slang. She peppers conversation with an appropriate "bloody" or two with the panache of an Eliza Doolittle. "Bloody" on Heather's lips can turn into an expression of glorious indignation.

"On the court," I once asked her, "do you think you've got the quality that athletes call 'killer instinct?'"

"Bloody right!" she answered.

Pride is another of her qualities, pride on and off the court. It shows in her clothes, which are unfailingly neat and stylish. And it shows in her regard for her record, her achievements and her continuing status in squash.

"The Australian newspapers got me cranky," she said one day in the spring of 1977 not long after she'd returned to Toronto after winning the New South Wales Open. "One of them said I was 'fully extended' in the finals at the tournament. *Fully extended!* I beat Sue Newman 9-5,

9-7, 9-1. I don't call that fully extended. Bloody hell, I'm not an old lady yet."

In late May of 1977, I had a rare chance to see for myself how far from an old lady Heather is, how fit and accomplished and inventive she remains on the squash court. I traveled with her and Brian to New York where Heather had agreed to play in a charity exhibition against Frank Satterthwaite, one of 1977's top American male professionals. The McKays arrived in New York a couple of days before the match, and spent their time like typical folks from out of town. They took a boat to the Statue of Liberty, rode an elevator to the top of Empire State Building and pushed their way through Blooming-dale's department store. Heather also subjected herself to some testing by the Sports Medicine Division of the Lenox Hill Hospital. The doctors put her legs through two hours of rigorous examinations and concluded that she had the strongest right leg of any woman they had ever encountered, much stronger than that of a famous ballet dancer who'd taken the same tests earlier in the spring.

The match against Satterthwaite was scheduled for early evening at the University Club, an elegant ten-storey building at Fifth Avenue and 54th Street. Inside, the club was stately with its marble pillars, high ceilings, ornate decor and its rows of stern portraits of ancient, wealthy and influential New Yorkers. A group of about sixty men, most of them dressed in conservative good taste and looking perfectly at home in the club's discreetly affluent atmosphere, gathered before the match (for which each had paid $100) in a drawing room on the fifth floor to sip drinks and handicap Heather's chances against a male pro. Frank Satterthwaite was there, a genial and thoughtful thirty-four-year-old from a well-connected New York family who earns his living by playing professional squash and writing books and magazine articles about sports. He ordered a Coke and explained why he was taking on Heather in a match from which he had little to gain and much to lose.

"Why play a woman at all?" he said. "Well, because I like to set myself challenges. When I'm finished with squash, I want to be able to say that I've gone against all the best players, no matter who they were. I played Hashim Khan when he was sixty years old. It was like playing a legend, the first great hero of squash and, I'll tell you, it was a struggle. I think playing against Heather is in the same category."

A half hour later, the crowd took elevators to the squash courts on the tenth floor and settled down in the gallery. The court for the match was American, smaller than the international court, but the ball was the soft international ball. It put Satterthwaite, who plays the hard-ball game that's native to the United States, at a disadvantage, though he more than compensated with natural superiority in weight, muscle and power. Frank's strength edge was clearly apparent when the two players stepped onto the court; while they were approximately the same height, Satterthwaite looked formidably stronger across the shoulders and chest. By comparison, Heather seemed almost dainty, an impression that was emphasized by her tasteful all-white squash dress embroidered with four wide light blue bands circling the bottom of the skirt. Around her neck hung a gold charm in the same design that she's worn since her first Australian Championship in 1960 — a four-leaf clover for luck.

The first game in the best-three-out-of-five match opened with long rallies, both players apparently content to drive the ball for length and wait on the opponent's errors. In this cautious way, the score crept to a 3-3 tie. Then Frank changed tactics, grew aggressive and went for nicks — low, hard, glancing and unreturnable shots into the front corners — and made enough of them to win with comparative ease, 9-3.

Heather began very quickly in the second game. She was stroking the ball more cleanly than Frank and showed more talent for placing the ball. Both of these qualities helped her get off to a 5-0 lead, and before Frank could collect himself, she had put the game away by a 9-3 score.

Game three was marked by errors, especially in the early minutes. Frank forced more of them than Heather, and he held leads of 6-3 and 8-5. But Heather's backhand, which she relied on throughout the match, was working its magic. She moved around the court with a dancer's agility and economy, and gradually she pulled even at 8-8, then 9-9. The game, stretching out to an exhausting twenty minutes, was decided with dramatic suddenness when a penalty point was called against Frank. His style was to crowd Heather, something common in hard ball. He stood close to her and made her play around him but, on the decisive point, he went too far in this tactic. He crossed in front of the ball just before a shot of Heather's and made insufficient effort to move out of her way. In hard ball, a let would have been called, but in soft ball it was a penalty point, giving her the game 10-9. She went ahead, two games to one.

Frank raced to even matters in game four. He hit his shots short and made them consistently good. There were no long rallies in the game, nothing that allowed Heather to get a foot in the contest, and Frank finished things off with a swift, convincing 9-1 win.

In the fifth and last game Frank was out in front 3-0 before Heather recovered the serve with a gorgeous forehand nick. She brought the score to 3-3. Then Frank asserted his power again and went up at 5-3 and 8-4. Heather fought back. She forced an error to make it 8-5. She retrieved Frank's shots relentlessly, forbidding him from making the final point of the match. The game moved to 8-6 and stalled there as the serve changed hands twelve times without a point being scored. The excitement and tension in the gallery were almost visible. Heather forced another error, and the score was 8-7. Once again, the serve moved repeatedly back and forth, each player taking turns saving point and recovering serve with thrilling desperation shots. Finally Frank took service on a perfect return of Heather's serve into the opposite corner and, in the long rally that followed he lunged for a frantic return from a spot behind the service box. His shot, on its way to the front wall, hit Heather and, by the rules, gave Frank the decisive point. He had the game, 9-7, and the match, three games to two. The gallery shouted cheers and bravos for both players.

Afterwards, a small party of players and fans adjourned to an Indian restaurant a few blocks away for a late supper of curry and cold drinks. Heather, looking a trifle wan, said that in any match against a good man player, the longer it lasted, the less chance she had of winning.

"No matter how fit I get myself," she said, shaking her head in a small show of regret, "the bloody man's always going to be stronger."

Satterthwaite smiled and offered an analysis of Heather's gifts, one superb player paying tribute to another.

"What you saw on the court tonight was a perfect illustration of the thing that's made Heather so great for so long — her absolute refusal to yield. Sure, she has all the natural equipment, all the shots, all the squash intelligence, all the know-how. She's got those in abundance. But then she has the extra, the incredible determination that transcends everything else. I thought out there in the fifth game when she started to come back in that unbelievable way that I would lose, and I'm certain that all of her opponents over the years, all those women she's defeated, have experienced the same kind of sinking inevitability. Heather will simply never quit, and that, together with her technical ability, makes her not just the all-time best woman squash player but probably the most fantastic woman player in any racket sport — tennis, badminton, squash — who's ever lived."

CHAPTER ONE

Getting Started: The Feel of Squash

I once said something to a reporter from the *Times* of London that still strikes me today as pretty sensible. It was in February 1966, just after I'd won against Anna Craven Smith, 9-0, 9-0, 10-8, in the finals of the British Championships at the Lansdowne Club in London. I was twenty-five years old and the win made my fifth straight British title. After the match was over, the *Times* reporter asked me why I kept on playing squash when, presumably, there were lots of easier or more lucrative activities I would be doing.

"I don't go on the court and slave," I answered. "I enjoy playing. I love the game — and that's why I keep at it."

Right. Love of the game — it's at the heart of everything about squash, not just for me but for anybody else who's already playing the game or who's thinking of taking it up. If you don't love squash, don't bother with it. If you get out on the court and find yourself in a constant foul mood, then forget about squash and give tennis a try — or maybe darts. You need affection for the game to enjoy it and to improve your skills. It may take you a month or a whole season of play before you can decide whether your relationship with squash is a love affair or a mutual dislike. But in any event you must go to squash prepared to give it your best efforts. Love of the game is where everything begins.

Mind you, it's sometimes difficult to love a game that can arouse your temper in as deadly a way as squash is apt to. I had my first experience of horrendous temper on a squash court very early in my competitive years, and it was a revelation. It happened in the semifinals of the New South Wales Junior Championships in 1960. I was the new girl from Queanbeyan, the nobody from nowhere who wasn't supposed to win anything, and when my opponent, who *was* supposed to win something, maybe everything, began to fall behind in the match, she blew up. The language was fierce. She lost her temper and she lost the match, a combination that often occurs at all levels of squash, among champions and beginners. The reason is that squash is such a fast sport, and when your temper gets the best of you, making you fret over a bad shot, then your opponent is likely to run off three or four quick points before you've recovered your poise.

I used to have my own trouble with crankiness. I broke rackets against the court walls when I was new to the game, and I turned the air blue with some choice profanity. I knew all the words. I grew up with five brothers and I could swear with the best of them. But I learned fairly soon that my nasty moods were hurting my game, and I learned to control them. The decisive moment in keeping my temper in check, in not even allowing it to be a factor in a match, came during a tournament in Melbourne in 1962. I was playing my opponent for a game point and in the middle of a rally, as I was going for a shot, she stepped on my foot and kept me from the ball. I thought at the very least I should have been given a let and allowed to play the point over again. But the referee, who happened to be my opponent's husband-to-be, ruled against me. I was furious. But instead of letting my control fly out the window, I just grew more determined to win, and I did. And that's the way I am today; if a referee's bad call goes against me or if I make a silly shot, I buckle down and become more dedicated to winning the next point.

PATIENCE AND CONCENTRATION

These are the weapons that squash players must cultivate to fight off a bad temper. Patience is essential — two different kinds of patience. First of all, you must have the patience to practice. If you're ambitious to make yourself a good strong all-round player, then you need the special patience that's required to step on to a court all by yourself and hit a ball up and down the side wall for twenty minutes. It takes infinite patience to master — or attempt to master — all the shots in the squash repertoire.

Then there's the entirely different kind of patience that you need for actual play against an opponent. In this case, it's patience that's based on one essential word — *don't*. Don't expect too much too soon from your abilities on the squash court. Don't suppose that you can put the ball exactly where you want it every time you hit it. Don't attempt to finish off a game too quickly when the circumstances aren't yet right for you to make it successfully. In many ways, you see, squash is a game of waiting. You have to wait until you've learned to control a shot before you can expect great things from it. You must wait during any given rally until your position and your opponent's position and the ball's position are all just right before you go for a winning shot, instead of trying to force the winner and polish off your opponent too soon.

As for concentration, it's something you can't afford to lose.

Concentration is the quality that Evonne Goolagong, the great Australian tennis player, has lost when she goes on one of her "walkabouts" during a match. Concentration means never relaxing. It means paying attention to whatever is happening around you at every moment. It's a crucial attribute in all sports, but concentration may be needed most of all in squash because, as I can't emphasize too often, it's a game that moves with such speed. A point can be won — or surrendered — in a flick of the eye.

A perfect example of loss of concentration came in the third game of that British final I played in 1966 against Anna Craven Smith. I beat her 9-0, 9-0 in the first two games and had her 8-0 in the third. Then foolishly I chose that moment to relax. She won a point. It was 8-1. Oh well, I thought, no harm done. In a few minutes, it was 8-2, then 8-3, then 8-4. The points had come to me quickly in the first two games and now they were leaving me just as quickly in the third game. I'd lost my concentration, and I didn't recover it until we were even at 8-8. At last, I remembered how to bear down once again, and I took the last two points for the 10-8 win. But it was a close call, one that I would rightly blame on loss of concentration.

There is a small trick that you can play on yourself to regain slipping concentration. You pretend you are in a slightly tough spot, that it's match point against you. Don't hit any stupid shots or take any risky moves. Pay strict attention to the business of playing good, sound, straightforward squash. It's a superficial trick perhaps but it generally helps heighten my powers of concentration.

FITNESS

Love of the game, patience and concentration are all very necessary ingredients to the squash player, but in a sense there's something even more fundamental, something physical, that is required. It's fitness, of course, the sort of good health which permits vigorous exercise. Certainly anybody who's just venturing into squash, especially those over thirty and past the age when they're regularly active in sports, should first get a thorough checkup from a doctor. If the squash club or athletic organization that the new player belongs to offers fitness testing, the kind that examines vital capacity, heart reserve and oxygen uptake, then by all means take advantage of the testing. The more we know about the body and its workings, the less inclined we are to abuse it.

Once medically cleared for action, a squash beginner or an older player or an infrequent player who plays fewer than a couple of games a week, shouldn't look for unnecessary challenges. The advice I give to such players boils down to this: you ought to play against an opponent who is roughly at the same level of ability. Don't play someone who's likely to run you around the court. That's asking for trouble; you'll be worn out and you might even feel discouraged from ever again stepping back on a squash court. Line up somebody of your own skills for a match, and when the two of you have played enough games to feel tired, then stop. Don't suppose that because you've booked a court for forty minutes you're obliged to stick it out for the whole forty minutes. If twenty-five or thirty minutes of squash leave you slightly ragged, then twenty-five or thirty minutes are plenty for you. Leave the marathon games to the club champions.

A SPORT FOR ALL AGES

Age isn't necessarily the decisive factor. I've met — and played against — many players in their fifties and sixties who are capable of excellent squash and who can keep up their high standards over four or five games. Squash is a game that any reasonably healthy man or woman can play into late middle age. To be sure, squash isn't a game that you should *start* in late middle age, unless you are in exceptional physical health. Almost all of the good older players I know are people who have been at squash over a long period of time and have refused to give it up just because they've passed retirement age. These older players maintain a regular playing relationship with two or three people who are at the same level of ability, and together they can continue to play for years. As a matter of fact, many veterans reach the point where they can outfox much younger opponents. The older players have it all in their heads, and they use racket skills, control of the ball and lots of wile and guile to whip the faster and fitter juniors.

At the other end of the age spectrum from the seniors, there is an increasing number of talented young people around the world who are discovering squash. I ran into one of them in the first round of the 1977 British Open. Her name was Ruth Strauss, she was from England, and she was only thirteen years old. Ruth hit the ball beautifully, but she didn't yet have the knack for setting herself up quickly enough to make a shot, and I was able to win the match, 9-0, 9-0, 9-0. Many squash clubs are very active these days in bringing along youngsters like

Ruth, though unfortunately many teenagers at least in North America don't start squash until they reach college at seventeen or eighteen. Personally, I think thirteen is the ideal age to start.

All the same, I have to say that I'm just as glad I didn't play squash myself until I was eighteen. Most of my generation of women players, it seems, began as late in life as I did. But we late bloomers are still at the game and still winning tournaments in our mid-thirties. I'm not sure what the moral is, except that younger beginners, boys and girls who pick up squash in their early teens, will need plenty of continuing encouragement from parents and coaches to stick at the sport. It's in the teens, after all, that a youngster's dedication is most likely to dwindle in favor of other attractions.

EQUIPPING YOURSELF FOR SQUASH

No matter what age a player starts squash and no matter to what age he continues to play, he must take care to choose and use his equipment with care and good sense.

Racket: I've played with a Spalding since my earliest days on a court. I bought the first one myself just by picking it out at a sporting goods store without really understanding what I was looking for. I broke that racket, and not long after, before I'd even played in a tournament, a man named Jack May from Sydney heard that I was a promising junior and sent me, free of charge, two Spalding Executives. As I played I gradually began to recognize the qualities in a racket that most suited my game and style. Basically I prefer a racket that's fairly light and isn't head heavy. Distribution of weight is important; it's possible to buy two rackets that weigh the same but to discover that one feels wrong because the weight is over-balanced in the head. I don't like a heavy racket that has a sort of dead weight and hefts like a lump of kindling wood in my hand. On the other hand, I'm not keen on a racket that's so light that I can barely feel it moving through the air when I swing it.

I also want a racket with a grip that's shaped in a rectangle. When I pick up a racket that has a round grip, my hand seems uneasy. I don't know where I am on the racket. But the rectangular shape reassures me. It fits my hand. It's natural. I can check the position of my hand on it quickly and easily and know that I'm holding it correctly. Years ago when I first decided on a rectangular grip, I couldn't find it, at least not in the style of racket that satisfied me, and my husband Brian used to spend a lot of his time shaving and shaping the handles for me. Eventually we got smart and one day after I'd broken one of my rackets, we sawed off the handle and shipped it to Spalding. The company took Brian's carving as a guide and began to manufacture a brand new model in my name with a rectangular handle. Some male players tell me that my model is slightly too light. But I reply that all the top players, men and women, favor a lighter racket; few of them touch the heavy models.

For those ambitious players who like to play in tournaments around their clubs or in higher competition, it's good advice to have more than a couple of rackets on hand at all times. Rackets have a bad habit of breaking during tough competition, as I discovered during my first visit to England in 1962. I'd reached the finals of the Scottish Championship against Eran Marshall, and in the course of the match I went after a ball that was close to the wall, overhit it and broke my racket on the wall. That happened twice, and because I'd only packed two rackets, the only way I could complete the match was to borrow a racket from a woman in the audience. It was embarrassing — doubly embarrassing because I lost the match. You can be sure that I've gone to every tournament since that Scottish Championship equipped with several rackets for every emergency.

Shoes: In my experience these are the features that I have decided are essential in a shoe meant to stand up to the wear and tear of squash: a wide last; a high arch support; and a heel that rises over the Achilles tendon.

Dress: There are one or two small tips I can make about squash clothing. Always wear a wrist band on your playing hand. It keeps the hand from getting too slippery, and you can also use the band to wipe perspiration from your forehead. For women, skirts are preferable to shorts because they cut down on restriction around the upper legs and allow you to stretch more comfortably to reach hard shots. Those are a couple of simple tips, but the main point I want to make about squash dress has to do with appearance and hygiene. Too many players think that because they're going to be sweating away on the squash court, then a pair of old shorts and a tattered shirt are suitable. They're wrong. What's more, it's impolite and undignified. All players should look neat and tidy -- at least they should when they step on to the court, even if they may get a bit disheveled after forty minutes of tough play. The rules of squash call for all-white outfits, but I think pastel clothing fills the bill, too. Good hygiene calls for frequent washing of squash clothes. Respect for the game and your fellow players dictates that you follow these suggestions.

BE A SPORT

Another way of showing respect is to observe the rules of good sportsmanship in squash. There are all sorts of sly ways that a player, if he has a small mean streak, may take advantage of an opponent. Player *A* (the mean fellow) can, for example, deliberately stand so close to Player *B* (the unluckly opponent) when it's *B*'s turn to hit the ball that *B* can only play a half-hearted shot. *B* is probably entitled to ask for a let in those circumstances, but too many players are reluctant to do so, and they're the poor chaps who get victimized by the bad sports. Another dirty trick some players pull when they're tired is to flick the ball away to a corner when it's their opponent's turn to serve. That delays the game a few seconds and gives the fellow an undeserved rest. I've seen top players in championships try this trick. I've also seen them argue needlessly with the referee in order to gain a few moments of recovery. I've seen them stall around in the change room beyond the legal between-games rest period. Naturally I don't recommend such behavior to any squash player, beginner, veteran or champion. Good sportsmanship is a key ingredient to the game. Bad sportsmanship, on the other hand, cancels out the quality that I think is at the very heart of squash — love of the game.

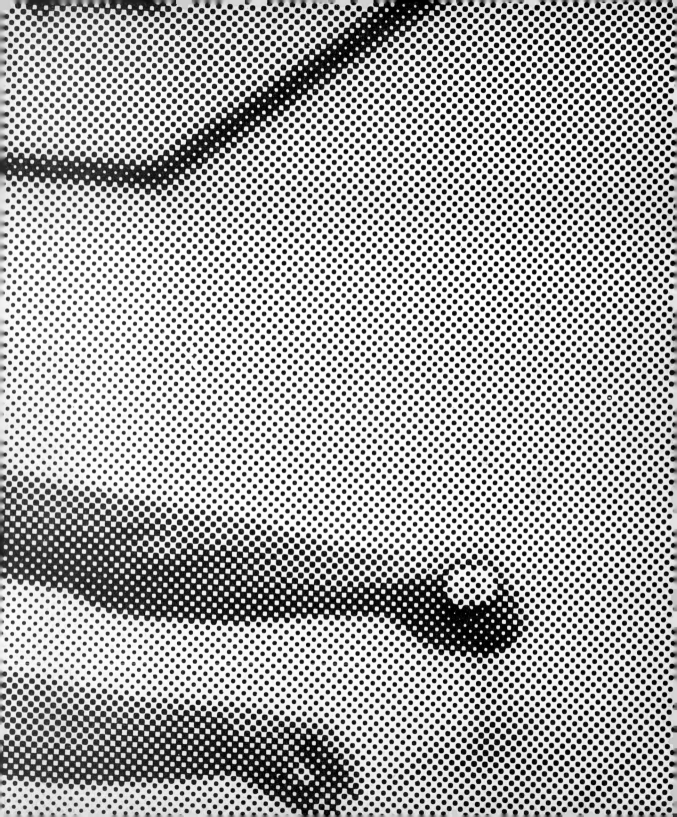

CHAPTER TWO

The Game: Terms, Rules and Courts

The history of squash dates back to the late nineteenth century. The game of squash as it was known in England, the land of its invention, first arrived in North America at the Montreal Racquets Club, then was passed on, via St. Paul's School in the town of Concord, New Hampshire, to the United States. That's when the Americans began to tinker with the English game with an eye to speeding things up. They made the court smaller, the ball harder and the rules more streamlined. Eventually the American modifications were adopted by Canada, Mexico and one or two other Latin countries, and the result is that the game as it's played in North America today is different from the game as it's played in the rest of the world.

The North American court is narrower than the English by two and a half feet and slightly less roomy in a couple of other minor ways. The North American ball is larger than the English ball and much harder. You can't squeeze it in your fist the way you can any of the softer international balls. It's tough and it's solid. So, owing to the hard ball and the smaller court, the North American game is faster than international squash.

In Canada, in recent years, the soft ball has grown increasingly popular. The Canadian Women's Squash Association adopted the soft ball as its official ball in the mid-1970s, and a great many Canadian men, in fact the overwhelming majority in several clubs, have chosen the soft ball over the hard as their preference for regular

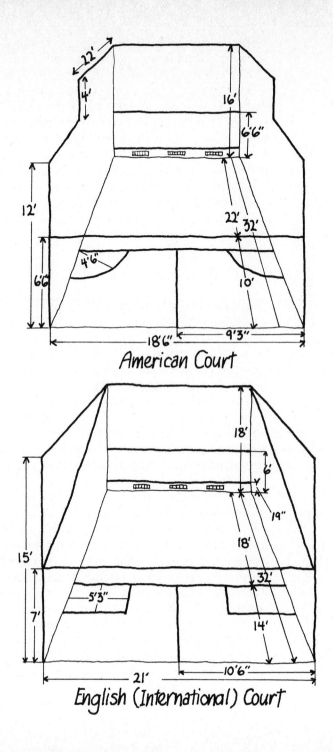

American Court

English (International) Court

matches. Since there are few soft-ball courts in the country, Canadians are playing with a soft ball on courts that were constructed for the hard-ball game.

The honest truth is that I really don't know or understand much about hard-ball squash. When a player at the Toronto Squash Club or anywhere else comes to me asking for a lesson in hard ball, I say, sorry, you'd best find another and better teacher. Hard ball is simply a different game, especially for someone — namely me — who grew up on the soft international ball.

For this reason, and for simplicity's sake, the information in this book relates to the English (International) court and the soft-ball game.

WHAT DO THEY PLAY?

For beginners at squash anywhere in North America, there's really not much harm in playing with the soft ball on a hard-ball court. Beginning and average players benefit from the slightly unorthodox arrangement because in a sense they have the best of both squash worlds. They're enjoying the slower ball on the smaller court. If they switched to the English court, they'd find it difficult to cover the extra few feet of floor space. And if they changed to the hard ball, then they'd run into problems in trying to chase down the ball's speedier flights.

But circumstances change with the better player, who's more likely to find that the soft ball on a hard-ball court adds up to a less interesting game. He'll find that he doesn't have the usual freedom of stroke that he has on the English court, and that he must cut down on his cross-court shots, which are among the game's more fascinating, since the smaller space makes it tougher to get the ball past an opponent with a cross-court hit. He'll feel more frequently crowded by his opponent, difficult to move his opponent out of the center of the court, because that two and a half feet less room means the opponent can more easily get to a ball from the neighborhood of the T. In all these ways, and others, the more advanced player is bound to come to the conclusion that the odd arrangement — soft ball on an American court — turns squash into a slightly less skillful and challenging game.

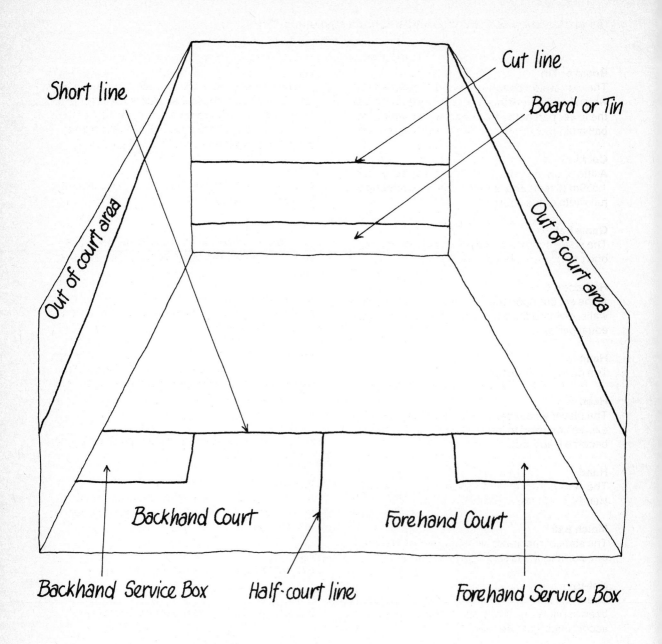

Short line

Cut line

Board or Tin

Out of court area

Out of court area

Backhand Court

Forehand Court

Backhand Service Box

Half-court line

Forehand Service Box

THE TERMS

(as provided by the International Squash Rackets Federation)

Board or Tin
The expression denoting a band, the top edge of which is .483m (19 inches) from the floor across the lower part of the front wall, above which the ball must be returned before the stroke is good.

Cut Line
A line upon the front wall, the top edge of which is 1.829m (6 feet) above the floor and extending the full width of the court.

Game Ball
The state of the game when the server requires one point to win is said to be "Game Ball."

Half-court Line
A line set out upon the floor parallel to the side walls, dividing the back half of the court into two equal parts.

Hand-in
The player who serves.

Hand-out
The player who receives the service; also the expression used to indicate that Hand-in has become Hand-out.

Hand
The period from the time when a player becomes Hand-in until he becomes Hand-out.

Match Ball
The state of the match when the server requires one point to win is said to be Match Ball.

Not-up
The expression used to denote that a ball has not been served or returned above the board in accordance with the rules.

Out
The ball is out when it touches the front, sides or back of the court above the area prepared for play or passes over any cross bars or other part of the roof of the court. The lines delimiting such area, the lighting equipment and the roof are out.

Point
A point is won by the player who is Hand-in and who wins a stroke.

Quarter Court
One part of the back half of the court which has been divided into two equal parts by the half-court line.

Service Box or Box
A delimited area in each quarter court from within which Hand-in serves.

Short Line
A line set out upon the floor parallel to and 5.486m (18 feet) from the front wall and extending the full width of the court.

Striker
The player whose turn it is to play after the ball has hit the front wall.

Stroke
A stroke is won by the player whose opponent fails to serve or make a good return in accordance with the rules.

Stop
Expression used by the Referee to stop play.

Time
Expression used by the Referee to start play.

There are, to be sure, efforts being made by various manufacturers and associations and squash devotees to bridge the American and international games. In parts of the United States, many players are experimenting with methods of slowing down the hard ball. In recent years, a new ball has come along, the 70 Plus, that includes some properties of both the hard and soft balls. The 70 Plus is the size of the smaller English ball, but more firm than the traditional English ball.

HARD VS. SOFT: TACTICS

My basic advice to soft-ball players is that they should stick to their own game and not monkey about with switches back and forth between hard and soft ball. Changing games is bound to leave a player less proficient in both. Maybe the best way to emphasize my point is to outline the four basic differences between international squash and American squash, the differences that make switching games so treacherous.

1. The stroke is different. This is partly because the racket is different in hard ball, heavier, more solidly built and strung with weightier gut. The racket, together with the faster nature of hard ball, means that the swing isn't nearly as big as in soft ball. In soft ball, a player takes his racket through the ball and then brings it up in the air. In hard ball, a player comes across the ball and cuts the swing short on the follow-through. The difference in swing applies to both the forehand and backhand, and it can wreak havoc with a soft-ball player who is shifting games.

2. The pacing and fitness are different. There's always been a continuing argument over which game calls for the finer degree of fitness. In soft ball, where you move around the court much more, you need stamina to hold up over the much longer rallies that are part of the game. In hard ball, the rallies are shorter, but they're also sharper and quicker because of the ball's speed. I, for one, find that I can recover more quickly from a short, snappy hard-ball rally than I can from a longer, more grueling soft-ball rally. Let's just say that both games demand keen fitness, but that international players need the sort of conditioning which will stand up to long sieges. As far as that goes, the longest soft-ball squash tournament match on record lasted two hours and thirty-five minutes. It's a rare event when a hard-ball match stretches out to half that length of time.

3. The rules are different. It's disconcerting, for instance, to go from the international game where you make points only on your serve to the American game where you can win points whether you're serving or receiving. Slight adjustments to your game strategy are required. On the more practical side, hard ball is a much more physical game. The thinking is that because the American ball makes for much faster action, the demands of the rules on a player to get out of his opponent's way aren't nearly as strict. More crowding is permitted, and there are far fewer lets and let points called in hard ball than in soft ball. The danger for the international player, if he dabbles too much in the American game, is that he's used to the bumping and crowding, and is penalized for these tactics when he reverts to soft-ball playing. He's also apt to find himself unpopular with his opponents.

4. The overall strategy is different. In general, hard-ball players use far more reverse angles than you'll ever see in international squash, and they hit low hard cross-court shots at every opportunity. On the other hand, they rarely try a boast from the back of the court, which is a regular working shot in the soft-ball game. The differences in shot selection are, once again, due to the nature of the ball, and they can be terribly confusing to an international player who's getting his first taste of them.

At the Bancroft tournament, my hardest game by far came in the semifinals against Gretchen Spruance who was the U.S. national champion. Why was it so tough? Simple: she stuck to hard-ball tactics. One shot she used to very good advantage, for instance, was a reverse angle which she'd hit when she was in front of me and a few feet out from the right side wall. It's a shot that I don't see much of in international games and it was tricky to handle. Gradually I adjusted to her approach and started to use some of the shots she was introducing to me in the course of the match. I played hard-ball squash, and I was able to come away with the win, 15-5, 15-10, 15-3.

CHOOSING THE RIGHT SOFT BALL

My first experience with the variations in soft balls came in the early 1960s when I began my trips to English tournaments. In Australia, we played with the yellow dot ball, but in Britain I was confronted with something called the Dunlop Butyl, a composition ball that was different from the yellow dot. The English ball was spongier and softer. It would hit the front wall, flatten out, then pop back into play at a much slower rate of speed than I was accustomed to with the ball at home. It didn't do me much good to hit the English ball hard — it would still flatten itself against the wall, and I found it a tough chore to get any length from my shots. I finally decided that the best bet was to slow down my game to control the ball, but I realized that I would always need a week or so to make the transition from the game in Australia to the game in England.

Eventually, by the mid-1960s, the English ball was playing the same as the Australian and still does. But the yellow dot isn't the *only* soft ball available for general play. There are also white dot, blue dot and red dot balls, with the colors denoting varying degrees of speed and bounce. That is to say, the blue and red are fast (and quite bouncy), the white is medium (less bouncy), the yellow is slow (even less bouncy). A further problem is that the same ball may perform with different speed and bounce on different courts. A squash ball is made of rubber and needs warmth to acquire its spirit, and therefore the same ball is almost certain to bounce with more verve on a court that's heated to 70 degrees Fahrenheit than on a court that's cooled to a chillier 55 degrees.

All of this adds up to an interesting study in the scientific properties of rubber, but to a squash player the information is more than mere technical data. It's important because the color of ball, and, thus, its degree of liveliness, is going to affect the nature of his play, particularly as he grows more skilled at the game. A couple of intermediate players who go on the court with a blue dot, for example, are bound to find themselves involved in a match that's full of abnormal bounces, wild ricochets and, in the end, general chaos. It'd be a better bet for them to ignore the blue dot in favor of the yellow and the more orderly and conventional game that goes with it.

RULES OF THE GAME

International Rules (as provided by the International Squash Rackets Federation)

1. The Game, how played
The game of Squash Rackets is played between two players with standard rackets, with balls officially approved by I.S.R.F. and in a rectangular court of standard dimensions, enclosed on all four sides.

2. The Score
A match shall consist of the best of three or five games at the option of the promoters of the competition. Each game is 9 points up; that is to say, the player who first wins 9 points wins the game, except that, on the score being called 8-all for the first time, Hand-out may choose, before the next service is delivered, to continue the game to 10, in which case the player who first scores two more points wins the game. Hand-out must in either case clearly indicate his

choice to the Marker, if any, and to his opponent.
Note to Referees
If Hand-out does not make clear his choice before the next service, the Referee shall stop play and require him to do so.

3. Points, how scored
Points can only be scored by Hand-in. When a player fails to serve or to make a good return in accordance with the rules, the opponent wins the stroke. When Hand-in wins a stroke, he scores a point; when Hand-out wins a stroke, he becomes Hand-in.

4. The Right to Serve
The right to serve first is decided by the spin of a racket. Thereafter the server continues to serve until he loses a stroke, when his

opponent becomes the server, and so on throughout the match.

5. Service

The ball before being struck shall be dropped or thrown in the air and shall not touch the walls or floor. The ball shall be served direct on to the front wall, so that on its return, unless volleyed, it would fall to the floor in the back quarter of the court opposite to the server's box from which the service has been delivered.

At the beginning of each game and of each hand, the server may serve from either box, but after scoring a point he shall then serve from the other, and so on alternately as long as he remains Hand-in or until the end of the game. If the server serves from the wrong box, there shall be no penalty and the service shall count as if served from the correct box, except that Hand-out may, if he does not attempt to take the service, demand that it be served from the other box.

A player with the use of only one arm may utilize his racket to project the ball into the air.

6. Good Service

A service is good which is not a fault or which does not result in the server serving his hand-out in accordance with Rule 9. If the server serves one fault, he shall serve again.

7. Fault

A service is a fault (unless the server serves his hand-out under Rule 9):

(a) If the server fails to stand with at least one foot on the floor within, and not touching the line surrounding the service box at the moment of striking the ball (called a foot-fault).

(b) If the ball is served on to, or below, the cut line.

(c) If the ball served first touches the floor on, or in front of, the short line.

(d) If the ball served first touches the floor outside the quarter of the court permitted for a good service in Rule 5.

8. Fault, if taken

Hand out may take a fault. If he attempts to do so, the service thereupon becomes good and the ball continues to play. If he does not attempt to do so, the ball shall cease to be in play, provided that, if the ball, before it bounces twice upon the floor, touches the server or anything he wears or carries, the server shall lose the stroke.

9. Serving Hand-out

The server serves his hand-out and loses the stroke:

(a) If the ball is served on to, or below, the board, or out, or against any part of the court before the front wall.

(b) If the ball is not dropped or thrown in the air, or touches the wall or floor before being struck, or if he fails to strike the ball, or strikes it more than once.

(c) If he serves two consecutive faults.

(d) If the ball, before it has bounced twice upon the floor, or has been struck by his opponent, touches the server or anything he wears or carries.

10. Let

A let is an undecided stroke, and the service or rally, in respect of which a let is allowed, shall not count and the server shall serve again from the same box. A let shall not annul a previous fault.

11. The Play

After a good service has been delivered, the players return the ball alternately until one or other fails to make a good return, or the ball otherwise ceases to be in play in accordance with the rules.

12. Good Return

A return is good if the ball, before it has bounced twice upon the floor, is returned by the striker on to the front wall above the board, without touching the floor or any part of the striker's body or clothing, provided the ball is not hit twice or out.

Note to Referees:

It shall not be considered a good return if the ball touches the board before or after it hits the front wall.

13. Strokes, how won

A player wins a stroke:

(a) Under Rule 9.
(b) If the opponent fails to make a good return of the ball in play.
(c) If the ball in play touches his opponent or anything he wears or carries, except as is otherwise provided by Rules 14 and 15.
(d) If a stroke is awarded by the Referee as provided for in the Rules.

14. Hitting an Opponent with the Ball

If an otherwise good return of the ball has been made, but before reaching the front wall it hits the striker's opponent, or his racket, or anything he wears or carries, then:

(a) If the ball would have made a good return and would have struck the front wall without first touching any other wall, the striker shall win the stroke, except that, if the striker shall have followed the ball round, and so turned, before playing the ball, a let shall be allowed.
(b) If the ball would otherwise have made a good return, a let shall be allowed.
(c) If the ball would not have made a good return, the striker shall lose the stroke. The ball shall cease to be in play, even if it subsequently goes up.

15. Further Attempts To Hit the Ball

If the striker strikes at, and misses the ball, he may make further attempts to return it. If, after being missed, the ball touches his opponent, or his racket, or anything he wears or carries, then:

(a) If the striker would otherwise have made a good return, a let shall be allowed.
(b) If the striker could not have made a good return, he loses the stroke.
If any such further attempt is successful, but the ball, before reaching the front wall, hits the striker's opponent, or his racket, or anything he wears or carries, a let shall be allowed, and Rule 14a shall not apply.

16. Appeals

(a) An appeal may be made against any decision of the Marker, except for (b) (i) and (ii) below.
(b) (i) No appeal shall be made in respect of foot-faults
(ii) No appeal shall be made in respect of the Marker's call of 'fault' to the first service.
(iii) If the Marker calls 'fault' to the second service, the server may appeal, and if the decision is reversed, a let shall be allowed.
(iv) If the Marker allows the second

service, Hand-out may appeal, either immediately, or at the end of the rally, if he has played the ball, and if the decision is reversed, Hand-in becomes Hand-out.

(v) If the Marker does not call 'fault" to the first service, Hand-out may appeal that the service was a fault, provided he makes no attempt to play the ball. If the Marker does not call 'Out' or 'Not Up' to the first service, Hand-out may appeal, either immediately or at the end of the rally, if he has played the ball. In either case, if the appeal is disallowed, Hand-out shall lose the stroke.

(c) An appeal under Rule 12 shall be made at the end of the rally.

(d) In all cases where an appeal for a let is desired, this appeal shall be made by addressing the Referee with the words 'Let, please.' Play shall thereupon cease until the Referee has given his decision.

(e) No appeal may be made after the delivery of a service for anything that occurred before that service was delivered.

17. Fair View and Freedom To Play the Ball

(a) After playing a ball, a player must make every effort to get out of his opponent's way. That is:

(i) A player must make every effort to give his opponent a fair view of the ball, so that he may sight it adequately for the purpose of playing it.

(ii) A player must make every effort not to interfere with, or crowd, his opponent in the latter's attempt to get to, or play, the ball.

(iii) A player must make every effort to allow his opponent, as far as the latter's position permits, freedom to play the ball directly to the front wall, or side walls near the front wall.

(b) If any such form of interference has occurred, and, in the opinion of the Referee, the player has not made every effort to avoid causing it, the Referee shall on appeal, or without waiting for an appeal, award the stroke to his opponent.

(c) However, if interference has occurred, but in the opinion of the Referee the player has made every effort to avoid causing it, the Referee shall on appeal, or may without waiting for an appeal, award a let, except that if his opponent is prevented from making a winning return by such interference or by distraction from the player, the Referee shall award the stroke to the opponent.

(d) When, in the opinion of the Referee, a player refrains from playing the ball, which, if played, would clearly and undoubtedly have won the rally under the terms of Rule 14(a) he shall be awarded the stroke.

Notes to Referees:

(i) The practice of impeding an opponent in his efforts to play the ball by crowding or obscuring his view, is highly detrimental to the game, and Referees should have no hesitation in enforcing paragraph (b) above.

(ii) The words 'interfere with' in (a) (ii) above must be interpreted to include the case of a player having to wait for an excessive swing of his opponent's racket.

18. Let, when allowed

Notwithstanding anything contained in these rules, and provided always that the striker could have made a good return:

(a) A let may be allowed:

(i) If, owing to the position of the striker,

his opponent is unable to avoid being touched by the ball before the return is made.

Note to Referees:

This rule shall be construed to include the cases of the striker whose position in front of his opponent makes it impossible for the latter to see the ball, or who shapes as if to play the ball and changes his mind at the last moment, preferring to take the ball off the back wall, the ball in either case hitting his opponent, who is between the striker and the back wall. This is not, however, to be taken as conflicting in any way with the Referee's duties under Rule 17.

(ii) If the ball in play touches any article lying in the court.

(iii) If the striker refrains from hitting the ball owing to a reasonable fear of injuring his opponent.

(iv) If the striker, in the act of playing the ball, touches his opponent.

(v) If the Referee is asked to decide an appeal and is unable to do so.

(vi) If a player drops his racket, calls out or in any other way distracts his opponent, and the Referee considers that such occurrence has caused the opponent to lose the stroke.

(b) A Let shall be allowed:

(i) If Hand-out is not ready and does not atthmpt to take the service.

(ii) If a ball breaks during play.

(iii) If an otherwise good return has been made, but the ball goes out of court on its first bounce.

(iv) As provided for in Rules 14, 15, 16(b) (iii), 23 and 24.

(c) No let shall be allowed when a player has made an attempt to play the ball except as provided for under Rules 15, 18 (a) (iv), 18 (b) (ii), and 18 (b) (iii).

(d) Unless an appeal is made by one of the player, no let shall be allowed except where these rules definitely provide for a let, namely Rules 14 (a) and (b), 17 and 18 (b) (ii) and (iii).

19. New Ball

At any time, when the ball is not in actual play, a new ball may be substituted by mutual consent of the players, or, on appeal by either player, at the discretion of the Referee.

20. Knock-up

(a) The Referee shall allow on the court to play to either player, or to the two players together, a period not exceeding five minutes, or two and a half minutes each, immediately preceding the start of play for the purpose of knocking-up. In the event of a separate knock-up, the choice of knocking-up first shall be decided by the spin of a racket. The Referee shall allow a further period for the players to warm the ball up if the match is being resumed after a considerable delay.

(b) Where a new ball has been substituted under rule 18 (b) (ii) or 19, the Referee shall allow the ball to be knocked-up to playing condition. Play shall resume on the direction of the Referee, or prior mutual consent of the players.

(c) Between games the ball shall remain on the floor of the court in view and knocking-up shall not be permitted except by mutual consent of the players.

21. Play in a Match Is To Be Continuous

After the first service is delivered, play shall be continuous so far as is practical, provided that:

(a) At any time play may be suspended owing to bad light or other circumstances beyond the control of the players, for such period as the Referee shall decide. In the event of play being suspended for the day, the match shall start afresh, unless both players agree to the contrary.

(b) The Referee shall award a game to the opponent of any player, who, in his opinion, persists after due warning, in delaying the play in order to recover his strength or wind, or for any other reason.

(c) An interval of one minute shall be permitted between games and of two minutes between the fourth and fifth games of a five-game match. A player may leave the court during such intervals, but shall be ready to resume play at the end of the stated time. When ten seconds of the interval permitted between games are left, the Marker shall call 'Ten seconds' to warn the players to be ready to resume play. Should either player fail to do so when required by the Referee, a game may be awarded to his opponent.

(d) In the event of an injury, the Referee may require a player to continue play or concede the match, except where the injury is contributed to by his opponent, or where it was caused by dangerous play on the part of the opponent. In the former case, the Referee may allow time for the injured player to receive attention and recover, and in the latter, the injured player shall be awarded the match under Rule 24 (c) (ii).

(e) In the event of a ball breaking, a new ball may be knocked-up, as provided for in Rule 20 (b).

Notes to Referees:

(i) In allowing time for a player to receive attention and recover, the Referee should ensure that there is no conflict with the obligation of a player to comply with Rule 21 (b), that is, that the effects of the injury are not exaggerated and used as an excuse to recover strength or wind.

(ii) The Referee should not interpret the words "contributed to' by the opponent to include the situation where the injury to the player is a result of that player occupying an unnecessarily close position to his opponent.

22. Control of a Match

A match is normally controlled by a Referee, assisted by a Marker. One person may be appointed to carry out the functions of both Referee and Marker. When a decision has been made by a Referee, he shall announce it to the players and the Marker shall repeat it with the subsequent score.

Up to one hour before the commencement of a match either player may request a Referee or Marker other than appointed, and this request may be considered and a substitute appointed. Players are not permitted to request any such change after the commencement of a match, unless both agree to do so. In either case the decision as to whether an official is to be replaced or not must remain in the hands of the Tournament Referee, where applicable.

23. Duties of Marker

(a) The Marker calls the play and the score, with the server's score first. He shall call 'Fault', 'Foot-fault', 'Out' or 'Not up' as appropriate.

(b) If in the course of play the Marker calls 'Not up' or 'Out' or in the case of a second service 'Fault' or 'Foot-fault' then the rally shall cease.

(c) If the Marker's decision is reversed on appeal, a let shall be allowed, except as provided for in Rule 24 (b) (iv) and (v).

(d) Any service or return shall be considered good unless otherwise called.

(e) After the server has served a fault, which has not been taken, the Marker shall repeat the score and add the words 'One fault,' before the server serves again. This call should be repeated should subsequent rallies end in a let, until the point is finally decided.

(f) When no Referee is appointed, the Marker shall exercise all the powers of the Referee.

(g) If the Marker is unsighted or uncertain, he shall call on the Referee to make the relevant decision; if the latter is unable to do so, a let shall be allowed.

24. Duties of Referee

(a) The Referee shall award Lets and Strokes and make decisions where called for by the rules, and shall decide all appeals, including those against the Marker's calls and decisions. The decision of the Referee shall be final.

(b) He shall in no way intervene in the Marker's calling except:

(i) Upon appeal by one of the players.

(ii) As provided for in Rule 17.

(iii) When it is evident that the score has been incorrectly called, in which case he should draw the Marker's attention to the fact.

(iv) When the Marker has failed to call the ball 'Not up' or 'Out,' and on appeal he rules that such was in fact the case, the stroke should be awarded accordingly.

(v) When the Marker has called 'Not up' or 'Out,' and on appeal he rules that this was not the case, a Let shall be allowed except that if in the Referee's opinion, the Marker's call had interrupted an undoubted winning return, he shall award the stroke accordingly.

(vi) The Referee is responsible that all times laid down in the rules are strictly adhered to.

(c) In exceptional cases, the Referee may order:

(i) A player who has left the court to play on.

(ii) A player to leave the court and to award the match to the opponent.

(iii) A match to be awarded to a player whose opponent fails to be present in court within ten minutes of the advertised time of play.

(iv) Play to be stopped in order to warn that the conduct of one or both of the players is leading to an infringement of the rules. A Referee should avail himself of this rule as early as possible when either player is showing a tendency to break the provisions of Rule 17.

(d) If after a warning a player continues to contravene Rule 20 (c) the Referee shall award a game to the opponent.

25. Colour of Players' Clothing

For amateur events under the control of the I.S.R.F. players are required to wear all white clothing provided, however, the I.S.R.F. officers at their sole discretion can waive compliance with this rule.

48

North American Rules (as provided by the United States Squash Rackets Association)

1. Server
At the start of a match the choice to serve or receive shall be decided by the spin of a racket. The server retains the serve until he loses a point, in which event he loses the serve.

2. Service
(a) The server, until the ball has left the racket from the service, must stand with at least one foot on the floor within and not touching the line surrounding the service box and serve the ball onto the front wall above the service line and below the 16' line before it touches any other part of the court, so that on its rebound (return) it first strikes the floor within, but not touching, the lines of the opposite service court, either before or after touching any other wall or walls within the court. A ball so served is a good service, otherwise it is a Fault.

(b) If the first service is a Fault, the server shall serve again from the same side. If the server makes two consecutive Faults, he loses the point. A service called a Fault may not be played, but the receiver may volley any service which has struck the front wall in accordance with this rule.

(c) At the beginning of each game, and each time there is a new server, the ball shall be served by the winner of the previous point from whichever service box the server elects and thereafter alternately until the service is lost or until the end of the game. If the server serves from the wrong box there shall be no penalty and the service shall count as if served from the correct box, provided,

however, that if the receiver does not attempt to return the service, he may demand that it be served from the other box, or if, before the receiver attempts to return the service, the Referee calls a Let (See Rule 9), the service shall be made from the other box.

(d) A ball is in play from the moment at which it is delivered in service until (1) the point is decided; (2) a Fault, as defined in 2 (a) is made; or (3) a Let or Let Point occurs (See Rules 9 and 10).

3. Return of Service and Subsequent Play
(a) A return is deemed to be made at the instant the ball touches the racket of the player making the return. To make a good return of a service or of a subsequent return the ball must be struck on the volley or before it has touched the floor twice, and reach the front wall on the fly above the tell-tale and below the 16' line, and it may touch any wall or walls within the court before or after reaching the front wall. On any return the ball may be struck only once. It may not be "carried" or "double-hit."

(b) If the receiver fails to make a good return of a good service, the server wins the point. If the receiver makes a good return of service, the players shall alternate making returns until one player fails to make a good return. The player failing to make a good return loses the point.

(c) Until the ball has been touched or has hit the floor twice, it may be struck at any number of times.

(d) If at any time after a service the ball hits outside the playing surfaces of the court playing surfaces of the court), the player so hitting the ball loses the point, unless a Let or a Let Point occurs. (See Rules 9 and 10).

4. Score
Each point won by a player shall add one to his score.

5. Game
The player who first scores fifteen points wins the game excepting that:
(a) At "thirteen all" the player who has first reached the score of thirteen must elect one of the following before the next serve:
(1) Set to five points — making the game eighteen points.
(2) Set to three points — making the game sixteen points.
(3) No set, in which event the game remains fifteen points.
(b) At "fourteen all" provided the score has not been "thirteen all" the player who has first reached the score of fourteen must elect one of the following before the next serve:
(1) Set to three points — making the game seventeen points.
(2) No set, in which event the game remains fifteen points.

6. Match
The player who first wins three games wins the match, except that a player may be awarded the match at any time upon the retirement, default or disqualification of an opponent.

7. Right to Play Ball
Immediately after striking the ball a player must get out of an opponent's way and must:

(a) Give an opponent a fair view of the ball, provided, however, interference purely with an opponent's vision in following the flight of the ball is not a Let (See Rule 9).
(b) Give an opponent a fair opportunity to get to and/or strike at the ball in and from any position on the court elected by the opponent; and
(c) Allow an opponent to play the ball to any part of the front wall or to either side wall near the front wall.

8. Ball in Play Touching Player
(a) If a ball in play, after hitting the front wall, but before being returned again, shall touch either player, or anything he wears or carries (other than the racket of the player who makes the return) the player so touched loses the point, except as provided in Rule 9(a) or 9(b).
(b) If a ball in play touches the player who last returned it or anything he wears or carries before it hits the front wall, the player so touched loses the point.
(c) If a ball in play, after being struck by a player on a return, hits the player's opponent or anything the opponent wears or carries before reaching the front wall:
(1) The player who made the return shall lose the point if the return would not have been good.
(2) The player who made the return shall win the point if the ball would have gone directly from the racquet of the player making the return to the front wall without first touching any other wall.
(3) The point shall be a Let (see Rule 9) if the return except for such interference would have hit the front wall fairly and (1) would have touched some other wall before so hitting the front wall, or (2) has

hit some other wall before hitting the player's opponent or anything he wears or carries.

When there is no referee, if the player who made the return does not concede that the return would not have been good, or, alternatively, the player's opponent does not concede that the ball has hit him (or anything he wears or carries) and would have gone directly to the front wall without first touching any other wall, the point shall be a Let.

9. Let

A Let is the playing over of a point.

On the replay of the point the server (1) is entitled to two serves even if a Fault was called on the original point, (2) must serve from the correct box even if he served from the wrong box on the original point, and (3) provided he is a new server, may serve from a service box other than the one selected on the original point.

In addition to the Lets described in Rules 2(c) and 8(c) (3), the following are Lets if the player whose turn it is to strike the ball could otherwise have made a good return:

(a) When such player's opponent violates Rule 7.

(b) When owing to the position of such player, his opponent is unable to avoid being touched by the ball.

(c) When such player refrains from striking at the ball because of a reasonable fear of injuring his opponent.

(d) When such player before or during the act of striking or striking at the ball is touched by his opponent, his racket or anything he wears or carries.

(e) When on the first bounce from the floor the ball hits on or above the six and one half foot line on the back wall; and

(f) When a ball in play breaks. If a player thinks the ball has broken while play is in progress he must nevertheless complete the point and then immediately request a Let, giving the ball to the Referee for inspection. The Referee shall allow a Let only upon such immediate request if the ball in fact proves to be broken (See Rule 13(c).)

A player may request a Let or a Let Point (See Rule 10). A request by a player for a Let shall automatically include a request for Let Point. Upon such request, the Referee shall allow a Let, Let Point or no Let.

No Let shall be allowed on any stroke a player makes unless he requests such before or during the act of striking or striking at the ball.

The Referee may not call or allow a Let as defined in this Rule 9 unless such Let is requested by a player; provided, however, the Referee may call a Let at any time (1) when there is interference with play caused by any factor beyond the control of the player, or (2) when he fears that a player is about to suffer severe physical injury.

10. Let Point

A Let Point is the awarding of a point to a player when an opponent unnecessarily violates Rule 7(b) or 7(c).

An unnecessary violation occurs (1) when the player fails to make the necessary effort within the scope of his normal ability to avoid the violation, thereby depriving his opponent of a clear opportunity to attempt a winning shot, or (2) when the player has repeatedly failed to make the necessary effort within the scope of his normal ability to avoid such violations.

The Referee may not award a Let Point as

defined in this Rule 10 unless such Let Point or a Let (see Rule 9) is requested by a player.

When there is no referee, if a player does not concede that he has unnecessarily violated Rule 7(b) or 7(c), the point shall be a Let.

11. Continuity of Play

Play shall be continuous from the first service of each game until the game is concluded. Play shall never be suspended solely to allow a player to recover his strength or wind. The provisions of this Rule 11 shall be strictly construed. The Referee shall be the sole judge of intentional delay, and, after giving due warning, he must default the offender.

Between each game play may be suspended by either player for a period not to exceed two minutes. Between the third and fourth games play may be suspended by either player for a period not to exceed five minutes. Except during the five minute period at the end of the third game, no player may leave the court without permission of the Referee.

Except as otherwise specified in this Rule 11, the Referee may suspend play for such reason and for such period of time as he may consider necessary.

If play is suspended by the Referee because of an injury to one of the players, such player must resume play within one hour from the point and game score existing at the time play was suspended or default the match, provided, however, if a player suffers cramps or pulled muscles, play may be suspended by the Referee once during a match for such player for a period not to exceed five minutes after which time such player must resume play or default the match.

In the event the Referee suspends play other than for injury to a player, play shall be resumed when the Referee determines the cause of such suspension of play has been eliminated, provided, however, if such cause of delay cannot be rectified within one hour, the match shall be postponed to such time as the Tournament Committee determines. Any such suspended match shall be resumed from the point and game score existing at the time the match was stopped unless the Referee and both players unanimously agree to play the entire match or any part of it over.

12. Attire and Equipment

(a) A player's attire must be white except that a solid, pastel color shirt may be worn. The Referee's decision as to a player's attire shall be final.

In the absence of a Referee, if a player's opponent objects to a colored shirt, white shall be worn.

(b) The standard singles ball as specified in the Court, Racket and Ball Specifications of this Association shall be used.

(c) A racket as specified in the Court, Racket and Ball Specifications of this Association shall be used.

13. Condition of Ball

(a) No ball, before or during a match, may be artificially treated, that is, heated or chilled.

(b) At any time, when not in the actual play of a point, another ball may be substituted by the mutual consent of the players or by decision of the Referee.

(c) A ball shall be determined broken when it has a crack which extends through both its inner and outer surfaces. The ball may be squeezed only enough to determine the extent of the crack. A broken ball shall be replaced and the preceding point shall be a Let (See Rule 9(f)).

(d) A cracked (but not broken) ball may be replaced by the mutual consent of the players or by decision of the Referee, and the preceding point shall stand.

14. Court

(a) The singles court shall be as specified in the Court, Racket and Ball Specifications of this Association.

(b) No equipment of any sort shall be permitted to remain in the court during a match other than the ball used in play, the rackets being used by the players, and the clothes worn by them. All other equipment, such as extra balls, extra rackets, sweaters when not being worn, towels, bathrobes, etc., must be left outside the court. A player who requires a towel or cloth to wipe himself or anything he wears or carries should keep same in his pocket or securely fastened to his belt or waist.

15. Referee

(a) A Referee shall control the game. This control shall be exercised from time the players enter the court. The Referee may limit the time of the warm up period to five minutes, or shall terminate a longer warm up period so that the match commences at the scheduled time.

(b) The Referee's decision on all questions of play shall be final except as provided in Rule 15(c).

(c) Two judges may be appointed to act on any appeal by a player to a decisions of the Referee. When such judges are acting in a match, a player may appeal any decision of the Referee to the judges, except a decision under Rules 11, 12(a), 13, 15(a) and 15(f). If one judge agrees with the Referee, the Referee's decision stands; if both judges disagree with the Referee, the judges' decision is final. The judges shall make no ruling unless an appeal has been made. The decision of the judges shall be announced promptly by the Referee.

(d) A player may not request the removal or replacement of the Referee or a judge during a match.

(e) A player shall not state his reason for his request under Rule 9 for a Let or Let Point or for his appeal from any decision of the Referee provided, however, that the Referee may request the player to state his reasons.

(f) A Referee serving without judges, after giving due warning of the penalty of this Rule 15(f), in his discretion may disqualify a player for speech or conduct unbecoming to the game of squash rackets, provided that a player may be disqualified without warning if, in the opinion of such referee, he has deliberately caused physical injury to his opponent.

When two judges are acting in a match, the Referee in his discretion, upon the agreement of both judges, may disqualify a player with or without prior warning for speech or conduct unbecoming to the game of squash rackets.

CHAPTER THREE

The Basic Repertoire: Serves, Strokes and Shots

When I was eighteen and knocking a ball around the squash courts in Queanbeyan, I discovered a book. It was an instructional squash book given to me by the man who wrote it, Vincent Napier, who was probably the first Australian to make a detailed study of the game. In those beginning years, I didn't understand many of the basics of squash. All I knew was running and hitting, purely instinctive stuff, and it was the Napier book that enlightened me about how the game ought to be played. I read Napier so many times that I almost had his instructions down by heart and I know that my game gradually began to improve under his guidance. Napier's book proved to me just how much any squash player, even a beginner can absorb about the game from the printed page.

There's one qualification I ought to make to that general endorsement. The fact is that you can't learn everything there is to know about squash from one source. The game is far too tricky and complex. In my own case, I can point to all sorts of teachers and professionals who brought me surprising new pieces of squash wisdom along the way. I'd think that I had a grasp on the game, and then, often out of the blue, someone would show me something fresh, a way of making a shot or of figuring an angle that had never before entered my mind. I remember, for example, the first time I traveled to England in 1962 and I met Dadir, the great Egyptian player and coach. For three weeks, he played me two or three times a week, and he taught me about feet. *"Feet!"* he'd shout at me. "Get your feet in position!" He impressed on me that you must always hit the ball off your front foot, that the better your footwork becomes, the better your stroke will be. I've never forgotten his lessons just as I've never forgotten his voice shouting at me: *"Feet!"*

A couple of years later, I went to Keith Walker, a squash pro in Sydney who was the first teacher to make me do some serious thinking on the court. Keith emphasized that squash is a game of angles and rebounds, and if you make the ball hit at a certain point on the front wall while it's traveling at a certain speed, then it's almost inevitably going to end up at another certain point in the back of the court. If you plan your shot before you hit it, calculating the angles and the bounces, you can make it travel on the exact flight that's going to put your opponent in an awkward spot. It seems all so obvious when it's put down in black and white, but it was an eye-opener to me when I first started to carry out his strategic suggestions on the court.

There've been all sorts of Dadirs and Walkers in my life, teachers who have enlarged and refreshed my game. The point is that every squash player must absorb whatever he can from whatever qualified professional or coach he encounters. And that's the spirit in which I offer this book. It may not answer all your questions about squash, but it presents the ideas that I've developed about squash over the years, the ways of moving and hitting and thinking that have worked for me.

THE FOUR DO'S OF SQUASH

Before I get to the grip and the various shots, let me first lay down four short rules that I think you ought to store away for permanent safekeeping. These rules are relevant to all aspects of the game. Don't forget them. Whenever your squash seems to be going stale, dust off these four rules and check them against your action on the court. If you're violating any of them your game will suffer.

1. Keep your eye on the ball. Need I say more? Your stroke may be flawless, your footwork agile, and you may have the court sense of a wizard, but if you insist on focussing your eyes on the front wall when you're supposed to be hitting the ball, then all your wonderful talents are likely to reward you with nothing except a fluffed shot. You'll bang the ball off the wood of the racket. You'll miss the angles you've aimed for. You might even fan on a shot. Avoid these mistakes by watching the ball.

2. Remember that the power comes from your arm, not from your shoulders and certainly not from your body. A squash stroke isn't like a tennis stroke in which you often try to throw your whole body behind a shot in order to generate maximum power. There's no time for such pyrotechnics in squash. Throw your body into a shot and you'll be hopelessly off-balance and out of position to deal with your opponent's return. Besides, to hit with your arm means that you can drive the ball longer without getting tired. Players with a good stroke are able to hit the ball till the cows come home without running out of steam.

3. *Squash is a game of spots.* Spots on the side walls, spots on the front wall, spots in the corners, all kinds of spots. More than that, squash is a game of *personal* spots. There is, for example, a spot on the left side wall somewhere just behind the service line that belongs exclusively to you. It's the spot that you must hit on a backhand boast in order to drive the ball into the right-hand corner just above the tin. The exact location of the magic spot depends on you — on your strength and on the power with which you uniquely strike the ball. What you must do through practice and play and experience is learn your spot on the left side wall for the backhand boast. Eventually you've got to master your spots for all the different squash shots. The idea behind the game after all is not to hit and hope. The idea is to hit the ball so that it'll end up where you want it.

4. *Consider the ball and its position* when you hit it, its position, that is to say, in relationship to you and your body. It shouldn't always be in the same position vis-à-vis the body. In fact, there are three different and definite positions from which I like to strike the ball. Remember them. On a cross-court shot, you should hit the ball when it's in front of your front foot. On a down-the-wall shot, you should hit it when it's immediately opposite your front foot or ever so slightly ahead of the foot. And on a boast, you should hit the ball just after it's passed the front foot.

Once these four essential rules are indelibly etched in your memory, you are permitted to move on to the following discussion of the grip and the strokes, but not before.

The Grip

I'm in favor of using one grip for all shots. That's contrary to the practice and advice of a number of other professionals. Kevin Parker, an excellent squash teacher, says he has seven different grips including one that allows him to retrieve nearly impossible shots from the back corner. But I'm against varying the way a player holds his racket according to the shot he's making. I say that one grip will do the job for all shots.

There are plenty of advantages to the single grip. For one thing, if you're an ordinary player, a need to switch grips is only going to confuse you and cost you points. By the time you've fumbled your way from a forehand grip to a backhand grip to meet your opponent's shot, the ball will be long gone past you. Other grips, what's more, might cause you to stroke the ball incorrectly, to come over the ball or to slice it too much in confusion. Then, too, you're bound to feel more comfortable with one consistent grip, provided, of course, that it's the *right* grip. That single grip, once it has sunk in and become natural, will provide you with confidence and control, a perfect combination. One grip will enable you to make the best possible use of whatever ability you possess.

Hold the racket with the left hand at the top of the shaft close to the head and with the racket at right angles to the floor. (I'm assuming, by the way, that you're right-handed; if you happen to be left-handed, follow all instructions with the left-and-right indications reversed.) Next, reach for the handle with the right hand as if shaking hands with the racket. That's as good a way as any to come to grips with the grip.

As you shake, the V between the thumb and index finger should be slightly off center and to the left of the handle. The heel of the hand, meanwhile, is resting lightly on a spot just above the butt of the handle. It shouldn't be *on* the butt. Playing with a grip on the butt will cause serious blisters on the edge of the hand.

Now, to focus on the fingers, the index finger must be slightly spread, leaving a small gap between it and the other three fingers, which remain in a firm row. Don't leave gaps between those three. The thumb should come to rest across the handle and next to the middle finger. Where many players err is that they extend the thumb down the left side of the handle. This is wrong. Wrap it around the racket till it meets the middle finger.

That's it. V slightly to the left. Heel above butt. Index finger spread. Thumb next to middle finger. If all those matters are in order, then squeeze securely on the racket, and you've got your grip. It's a grip that'll enable you to exercise control over all shots. Footnote: The one variation that I'll concede in the fundamental grip comes when you have to play a shot from deep in a back corner. Then — at least when you've graduated in ability from beginning player to competent player — it's useful to shorten up on your grip. You hold the racket with the same arrangement of palm and fingers, but slip your hand further up the handle towards the head. In such a way, you'll be able to maneuver the racket more expertly in tight quarters.

The Serve

Beginners don't use the serve as a weapon. They ought to. The serve is the only time during a game when you have absolute control over all the circumstances of a shot. On a serve, you're running the show, and your opponent must

wait and take his chances with whatever you offer. You can make the serve an attacking shot, a winning shot. That's particularly true in women's squash because many women seem to have trouble hitting the high overhead ball which is what you must do on many service returns. Make your serves as tough and expert as possible. Don't regard them as just a method of starting a game.

Let's begin with the serve from the court's right-hand serving box. Stand with the right foot in the box and the left foot lined up in a way that aims the hips into the front left-hand corner of the court. Hold the ball in the left hand. There's a knack to this. The left arm must reach out just so, not fully extended but with the elbow bent at enough of an angle, so that the ball is held at slightly below breast level. The hand is pointing upwards towards the ceiling and the ball is resting at the end of the fingers, loosely balanced and ready to be tossed gently into the air.

Now switch focus to the right arm. The racket should be more back than up. That is to say, the right arm is slightly bent and the racket head is extended slightly upwards. The reason that the racket isn't held way up in the air, over your head, is that it's going to hit the ball from *underneath*. That's essential. The action on the hit begins when the ball is tossed up with the left hand. It isn't a high throw, nothing like a tennis toss, but more of a slight flip. On the other hand, it isn't a drop either; don't turn the hand over, palm facing the floor, and simply let the ball sink. Toss it, and at the same time, swing the racket up and under the ball. It's a firm but gentle stroke, not executed with any great show of power, and it's purpose is to make the ball strike the front wall of the court just under the top red line. The idea is to hit as close to the red line as possible. That calls for an accurate eye, and the fact is that if you get the ball within, say, two feet of the line, you're doing a good job. The ball should also hit roughly at the center of the wall.

The reason for this accuracy is easy to figure. If the ball hits the designated spot, then it'll angle off the front wall, high across court and down the side wall, skimming so close to the side, ideally, that your opponent will find it impossible to volley back a return. The ball will brush down the side wall, land on the floor behind the service box and bounce into the back wall. If everything works to perfection on the serve, your opponent won't be able to take it off the side wall and he'll find himself in trouble with the back wall. He'll be handcuffed, and you'll either take a point on the serve or force the opponent to make such a feeble return that you'll be in fine position to play a winner on your next shot.

The serve from the left-hand side of the court is performed along the same basic principles but with a couple of variations in execution. Once again, I like to stand with the right foot in the serving box and the left positioned in a line that points the hips into the opposite front right corner. Then make your stroke in the same way, tossing the ball lightly and coming up from underneath the ball with the hit. This time, however, the point at which you aim the ball is not the middle of the center wall but about two-thirds of the way across from left to right. A good way to calculate the exact point is to extend in your mind the side line of the right-hand serving box until it reaches the wall and there, at the point of intersection with the front wall, is approximately where you aim the ball. Except, of course, the height of your hit is once again as close to the top red line as possible. From that point of contact — near to the upper red line and two-thirds of the way across the front — the ball will skim down the side wall, bounce once behind the service box, pop against the back wall and leave your opponent in a very difficult hole. The position high on the front wall may vary slightly depending on the angle of your stance and the strength of your stroke. You may find yourself making necessary adjustments in the spot you aim at as your angle and your power change.

The Hard Serve

The serve I've just described is the serve that I recommend you use most of the time. But for a strategic change of pace, you should also throw in a hard serve from time to time. It'll keep your opponent off-balance and guarantee that he can't relax, confident that the same style of serve is going to come at him throughout the match. The idea is to make the opponent nervous. Keep him guessing.

To begin a hard serve, toss the ball head high, about an arm's length to the right side and slightly in front of your body. Now bring the racket around in the same motion that you'd use if you were throwing a ball overhand, keeping the face of the racket vertical. Get plenty of shoulder into the hit. That's the way you'll generate the power that gives the hard serve its zip.

Now for the catch. You can't just smack the ball at random. Not at all. The idea, as with the conventional serve, is to hit the front wall at a specific point. In the case of the hard serve, it's just above the cut line. From the right-hand serving box, you direct the ball at the center of the front wall, and from the left-hand serving box, you direct it at a point two-thirds of the way across from left to right. Those two target areas are consistent with the usual serve. The difference lies in the target *level,* which is as close to the cut line as possible. From that point, provided your aim is dead-on, the ball will rebound to a spot on the side wall just behind the serving box on the opposite side of the court and about a foot and a half off the floor. Maybe your opponent will pick up the serve with a volley before it hits the wall. If he does, then he's shown himself to be a very sharp player, but even so, he may manage only a weak return, which you'll have no trouble dealing with. On the other hand, if your opponent doesn't volley the serve, he's in serious trouble. Why? Because the hard serve, properly executed, will bounce off the side wall, hit the floor and die against the back wall. That'll take care of your opponent's chances to return the ball.

The Forehand Drive

The purpose of this shot is to hit for length. You want to make sure that you give the ball enough of a whack that it comes off the front wall and lands well behind the service box. Ideally, the ball will bounce once on the floor and into the back wall, where it'll conveniently die. To achieve this is largely a matter of finding the level on the front wall that you should aim for with your forehand drive. The harder you hit the ball, the lower on the wall you can aim since, with power, the ball will naturally bounce further down court. If you lack a hard shot, if your strength only allows you to launch a relatively soft shot off your forehand, then aim it higher on the wall. It's not much use trying to bust hell out of the ball at a point six inches over the tin and then have the ball land feebly at mid-court where your opponent will have no trouble banging back his return for a potential winner. Be realistic. Propel your forehand at the spot on the front wall that's going to do you the most good.

The ready position for the forehand finds you balancing nicely on your feet, facing slightly towards the side wall, concentrating on the ball, holding your racket in front of you with the head up, not down. Suddenly you realize that your opponent has hit his shot to your forehand. Here comes the big moment. The ball is probably coming off the front wall down the right side close to the wall. That calls for a forehand return all right, and you begin to swing into position.

As the ball approaches, step forward and toward the side wall with your front foot, the left. The back foot, your right, is behind and resting lightly on the floor. How far apart should the two feet be? There's no hard and fast rule; they should simply be far enough apart that you can maintain good balance. The most common mistake is that players stretch the front foot too far toward the side wall and thereby throw themselves off balance and cut

Forehand Drive

Set yourself up for the shot as early as possible with racket high, elbow slightly bent, wrist cocked. As the ball approaches, step smartly and aggressively into the shot. Shift your weight to your front foot and bend your right knee. In mid-swing, the butt of the racket is showing the way and should be pointed, on a slant, toward the floor. At the instant of contact with the ball opposite the front foot, keep your hitting arm almost straight and well out from the body.

down on their potential for power in the shot. The right leg, at the back, is kept fairly straight while the left leg, at the front, is definitely bent. Most of your body weight, after all, is shifting onto the left leg, and it's got to bend to accommodate the shift.

What about the rest of the body? Your head should be aligned almost directly over the left foot. Your left shoulder dips down in the same direction. Meanwhile you've taken your right arm back in preparation for your stroke? How far back? Far enough so that the right hand is level with your shoulder. The elbow is bent slightly, and the wrist is cocked both upwards and slightly backwards. The motion the right arm goes through in making the stroke is rather like the motion you make when you skip a stone across the top of a body of water. Maybe you can grasp it better if you consider the path that the butt of the racket follows on the forehand. This is the flattened section at the very end of the handle, the part where the racket's trade name is usually engraved. What the butt is doing is leading the way. Or at any rate it's out front and leading the descent of the racket for about two-thirds of the way from the top of the swing to the point of impact with the ball. If you watch any player properly executing a forehand, you'll note that the butt of the racket is aimed at the floor, though on a slant, and stays like that until about a third of the way from the moment of impact, when the wrist naturally turns into the shot.

Ball and racket meet at a point opposite the left foot. That's the point at which you'll get maximum strength out of your forehand drive. Lean into it. At point of impact, the arm should be straight. Keep the face of the racket slightly open, then follow through. The whole idea of the stroke, in order to hit the ball hard, is to generate racket-head speed, and that calls for a complete follow-through. At the conclusion of the stroke your hand should end up close to the height of your left shoulder. Don't wrap your arm right around your head. That's going too far and will leave you off balance. On the other hand, don't go suddenly limp-wristed as soon as you've hit the ball and allow your stroke to come to an abrupt conclusion. The part of your arm that bends during the follow-through isn't the wrist. It's the elbow.

As soon as you've nicely finished the follow-through, right hand at shoulder level, then get yourself ready for the next shot. Bring your racket back to the ready position. Move over to the center of the court. Keep your eye on the ball.

Of course, if you've pulled off a perfect forehand, there may not be another next shot for you. With talent and a dash of luck, you will have successfully buried your opponent in the corner where he's faced with an impossible return.

The Backhand

The purpose of the backhand is identical to the purpose of the forehand. You're driving to length. You're squeezing your opponent to the back of the court. You're trying for a shot that'll come off the front wall, land once on the floor behind the service box and promptly expire against the back wall. Once again, you must find the right level for you — relative to your strength and power — on the front wall. Since the backhand is less of a natural shot to most players and calls for a swing that is slightly more difficult, chances are that you're going to have to aim your shot rather higher on the wall than with the forehand. However, as before, it's a matter of practice, experiment and experience. Find your level and work hard at hitting it right on target.

At the beginning of the backhand, stand in the usual ready position. Balanced on feet, eyes on ball, racket held in front with its head up, body slightly towards the side wall. Here comes the ball to the backhand side. Step forward and toward the side wall leading with the right foot. The right leg is taking the weight and is bent at the knee. Left leg is kept relatively straight. Remember that you're going to hit the backhand off the right foot. Hitting off the correct foot is especially important to women players who aren't as strong as the men and who must therefore follow all the orthodox rules of proper hitting to compensate and get the maximum power out of all shots. Men are often strong enough that they can get

Backhand Drive

In preparation for the shot, take your racket well back, wrist cocked and elbow bent at a small and comfortable angle. Keep your head down to the ball — don't raise it and don't sneak any peeks at the front wall — and as you move into the shot, let your weight flow forward to your front feet. Stroke the ball away from your body with a motion that makes your arm almost straight at the moment when the racket head strikes the ball. Follow through with your arm high and slightly bent.

away with hitting off the wrong foot. Jonah Barrington, the great English player, for example, plays plenty of his shots off his back foot, something that no woman could get away with.

Once the feet and legs are in position, check the arms. The left is held away from the body, safely out of harm's way but giving a nice sense of balance. Take the right arm back with the elbow bent and slightly away from the body and with the wrist firm and cocked. The idea of the backswing is to bring the whole arm into play on the hit, not just the forearm. Take the racket well back, just about shoulder high, and then swing into the shot. As your arm descends into the hit, it should gradually straighten until, at the point of impact, it is absolutely straight. That impact, by the way, takes place at a point just opposite the right foot.

After you've hit the ball, you've got to follow through with a slightly bent elbow. Your racket hand follows the flight of the ball and finishes at shoulder level. As with the forehand follow-through, never take the racket too far around your head. You'll throw yourself off-balance and probably crown your opponent in the bargain.

For those who play golf, the backhand and forehand swings are not unlike golf swings except that the point of contact with the ball is different: opposite the front foot in squash, more between the feet in golf.

The Volley

I play a volley — that is, a shot that comes off the front wall or side wall and is struck before it hits the floor — from any point on the court, but I like to use it best when my opponent is behind me. When possible, I'll hit it off the opponent's cross-court shot, thereby probably catching him off-balance and tucking away a winner by surprise tactics. This is a real attacking shot, and it's a true volley if you like, the kind that you can set yourself for, concentrate on and execute with classically proper style.

During a game, you're going to find volleys forced on you when you aren't particularly planning on hitting them. Suppose, for instance, you're caught out of position

or in an awkward stance, and it looks as if your opponent's shot is about to fly off the front wall past you and nestle in a corner. Simply by reflex, you reach out and try for a volley. You have no other choice. It's a case of getting a return back at all costs or losing a point. That frequently happens when you're close to the front wall, and a frantic volley is all that's open to you. In those situations, style usually goes out the window and you have to rely on instinct and swift reflexes.

Now let's look at the intentional forehand volley, the one that you can plan and carry out with a bit of finesse. First, get set, which means that you move yourself into the same position as you'd take for a forehand drive. Take the racket back — but not too far. One of the keys to the volley is a short backswing. It's different from a smash where you use a full backswing. All right, short backswing with the wrist cocked, which means that you're holding the racket head above the wrist. As the ball comes toward you, your weight begins to shift from the back foot to the front, right to left. The arm comes forward and it is almost fully extended in order to give the volley lots of drive. And your racket head meets the ball just ahead of your body. Then you make a short and snappy follow-through. Where on the front wall should you aim the shot? For length, quite high, well above the cut line. Why? Well, for one thing, you're striking the ball when it's at shoulder height or higher, and for another by hitting the ball high on the front wall, you're going to get good length on your volley, which is one of the basic reasons for using it. One more thought on the length volley: try to keep the racket face open during the hit. For a slightly different sort of volley — the attacking short volley — you close the racket face and you hit the ball low on the front wall just above the tin.

The Backhand Volley

Now you're over on the left side of the court and you're faced with ideal circumstances for a backhand volley to length. It's tougher to execute than the forehand volley, but with some attention to detail and enough practice, you'll find the hang of it.

What's different about the backhand volley is that you've got to lay your racket back a bit. That is, you must carry your right elbow high and hold the racket in a way that keeps its head almost parallel to the floor. Hold your arm just so as the ball begins to approach you on the fly. Your hitting stance is the same as for a backhand drive. Now start your stroke, arm extended and swinging, racket head above the wrist. The idea in this volley, as in the forehand volley, is to get your whole arm into the act. That's the source of your power.

Meet the ball just ahead of your body, and then follow through. There are many possible errors in the backhand-volley follow-through. Don't let your wrist droop immediately after contact. That's a common mistake. Keep a firm wrist for the follow-through. Don't step quickly forward with your left foot. Leave your back foot, the left, in place till you've completed the follow-through by bringing your hand to about shoulder level. And don't try to hit the ball too hard when you're just beginning to master the backhand volley. Many new players go haywire on the swing, reaching for power they think must be lurking somewhere inside them. Don't overswing. Don't rush the learning process. A volley, especially a backhand volley, takes patience.

72

The Smash

The perfect scenario for the use of a smash goes
something like this. You've taken your opponent short
with a shot, perhaps a drop, and he rushes to the front.
He hits a lob, but in his hurry he gets away a weak lob
that flutters to you just in front of mid-court at a height
slightly over your head. That's the signal for you to step
in with your smash. It isn't a shot that you'll call on very
frequently in a game, but when you let fly with it, a
smash is great for the offense. It quickens the pace of the
game, forces your opponent to move faster and sends him
dashing for the back of the court.

You hit the smash in much the same style you'd use in
a tennis smash. Take the racket back so that it reaches
down behind your head. Some teachers of the smash
insist that you pretend you're scratching your back with
the racket. I disagree. Don't take the head back quite that
far. Step into the shot as you would a conventional
forehand with your front left foot stepping toward the
side wall and forward at the same time. Bring the racket
overhead with a fairly straight arm and make contact
with the ball a little in front of your head and a little to
the right side. Finish up with a fairly extended follow-
through.

Aim is important in the smash. If you aim the ball too
high on the front wall, it'll ricochet from that wall to the
back wall on a straight line and then to the floor in
excellent position for your opponent to sock a return.
Same thing happens when you aim too low. The ball will
come off the front wall and bounce in front of the short
line, where once again the opponent will have a chance to
chuckle over his good fortune. Properly aimed, the ball
should come from the front wall to a landing spot back of
the service box and hit low on the back wall, dying before
the opponent can get his racket on it. Or at any rate
forcing him to muster a difficult return. Obviously the
best area on the front wall to steer your smash lies
somewhere above the cut line, but the exact location
depends on your own strength and power and is
something you'll have to determine through practice and
experiment.

The Drop Shot

Once, years ago when I was starting to win tournaments, a top Australian squash player told me that I should try more drop shots. Right, I said and proceeded to follow his advice. Hmm, he muttered after he'd watched me for a bit, maybe you should forget about drop shots. The top Australian player wasn't telling me anything I didn't already know — my drop shots were dreadful and they still give me trouble to this day.

A drop shot is a shot that is guided into a front corner, hitting the front wall immediately above the tin, then the side wall, and falling to the floor. Or, in a slight variation, when a drop shot is struck close to the side wall, it can hit the front wall close to the tin and fall straight to the floor. A drop shot, in effect, drops dead. But, alas, there are at least three ways in which you can mess up the shot. One mistake occurs when you try to cut things too fine — try to hit the ball too close to the tin — and thus end up banging into the tin for an error. Another mistake lies in playing the drop shot at the wrong time. The temptation to wrap up a point with a quick drop can easily lead you astray. Properly, you should play a drop shot off your opponent's boast from a back corner; that makes sense because with the opponent caught at the rear of the court, your drop shot will be over and done with before he can move up for a reply. Or you should use a drop shot when your opponent, who is once again behind you, has hit a ball that lands at about the short line; a drop shot from you, to the opponent's woe, will catch him too far in the back court to muster a return. Those are the right circumstances for the drop shot, but often you find yourself trying it when your opponent is closer to the front of the court and is therefore in position to move in for a quick bash at your sad effort. And that suggests the third mistake in using a drop shot: hitting it too hard. If you give your shot a vicious smash, then it's likely to rebound out of the corner, off the floor and down the court so far that your opponent, whom you were expecting to trap at the back of the court, has no trouble coming up with a return.

Now let's forget about the mistakes and move along to

Forehand Drop Shot
Get down to the ball — that's the key to a perfectly executed drop shot. From the very beginning of the stroke, set yourself in a semi-crouch. Carry the racket lower than you would for a drive, and move yourself into the shot, weight shifting to the front foot, closer to the floor than on the drive. Make contact with the ball slightly ahead of your front foot. Follow through smoothly. Don't stint on the follow-through. Don't pull your arm short. Let the stroke complete itself naturally.

the correct way to execute this devil of a shot. First, the forehand drop shot. Play it from the front of the court. A drop shot attempted behind the center of the court is almost always a risky enterprise. Don't bother trying one unless you're super expert at the shot — or unless your opponent is slow-footed. On the drop, the positioning of your feet is important. Line them up so that from back to front, right foot to left foot, they form a line pointing roughly into the right front corner. Now crouch. Bend your knees. This is a shot you've got to get well down to. Low, low, low — if you stand upright, you'll flub the shot for certain. Crouch, knees bent, feet in line to corner and, last but not least, weight on the front foot.

So much for the stance. Take a short backswing. Some coaches advocate a long backswing, arguing that you're thereby going to fool your opponent about your intentions for the ball. Don't bother. For most, the drop shot is a tricky enough maneuver without throwing in distraction tactics. The short backswing offers you comfort and confidence, and they're essential to the drop shot because it, of all strokes, is supposed to be the essence of smoothness, ease and control. There's nothing ferocious about it. Indeed, it's a very civilized sort of stroke. Keep the face of the racket open and stroke firmly through the ball, making contact between racket and ball at a point to the front of your left foot. And make sure you aim the ball away from the side wall and on to the front wall in order to achieve the necessary front wall-side wall angle.

Follow through. A frequent mistake is to stop the stroke abruptly after contact has been made with the ball. That's a sure way to knock the ball straight into the tin. Another warning: don't move your feet until you've completed the follow-through. You feel a terrible temptation to rush away before you've fully executed the shot. Resist. Hold your feet firmly in place until your racket has reached a point in the follow-through that brings its grip to about waist level. Once that's done, you can hustle away from the ball back towards the center in order to clear a path for your opponent, who is undoubtedly storming in from the back of the court in an effort to rescue the situation.

On the backhand drop shot, the principles remain the

Backhand Drop Shot

Move into the ball with your racket held back and low, at least lower than on a drive. Keep yourself down to the ball, and as you stroke it, reach out to make contact with the ball at a point just a little to the front of your front foot. Stay down to the shot — head down, body crouched, eyes focussed downwards on the ball — until you've come to the very end of the stroke. If you pull up short at any stage of the shot, you'll bang the ball into the tin.

same for execution. Feet lined up so that they point, back to front, left to right, into the left front corner. Knees bent. Weight on right foot. Body crouched. Short backswing followed by controlled and deliberate stroke that gets you right down to the ball. Contact with ball in front of right foot. Fairly short follow-through — and then a quick move out of the way.

One final tip. Occasionally you'll discover at the last instant that the ball is going to land too far in front of you for a sure drop shot, and on those occasions, you can try a little bit of deception on your opponent without much effort. Instead of stroking a drop shot, hit the ball cross court to the opposite corner or else lob it high on the front wall and into the back of the court. You can work those shots off both the forehand and backdrop drop shot, and since your opponent has already begun adjusting himself to deal with a drop shot, he's bound to suffer from the resulting double cross.

The Boast

Squash is a game of angles, and there's no shot that makes more use of angles than the boast. You hit it from a spot away from either side wall and from any place on the court, and you hit it in such a way that the ball bangs off the nearest side wall, zips diagonally across the court to a point low in the opposite corner at the front, striking in rapid succession the front wall and floor, dying against the side wall. The boast is a solidly defensive shot. It rescues you from the potentially awkward situation of dealing with a ball that's threatening to bound around a back corner, and at the same time it moves your opponent to the front of the court, thereby setting him up for a possible drive to length on your next shot. But it can also turn into an attacking tool. Suppose your opponent is somewhere deep in the back court. Then a good boast might catch him too far out of position to hit a return before the ball expires on the floor. Or, failing that, it might rush him into a flubbed return that you can easily take care of.

Let's look first at the backhand boast, the one that's hit from the left side of the court. Fundamentally, the area where you most often use it, at least as an attacking shot, is in the general area of the short line. What you're going to do is bang the ball off the left side wall and send it zipping into the right front corner, confounding your opponent in the process. Now, on this mid-court boast, get down to the ball as you would for a backhand drive. In fact, the stroke for the boast is just about identical to the stroke for the backhand drive. But there are a couple of differences. One is that this particular drive is directed at the side wall rather than the front wall. Another difference is that you make contact between racket and ball at a point just back of the right foot rather than, as in the drive, at a point opposite the foot. Step into the ball and drive it at the side wall, keeping the racket face slightly open. The target area on the side wall is crucial. It should hit that wall at a point ahead of your body and at a height that would be roughly between your knees and hips if you were standing upright. A ball hit at that angle and at that height will almost certainly follow the route you want — a line straight into the opposite front corner. If you hit it any lower on the side wall, it'll never reach the front wall before it strikes the floor or the tin. If you hit it any higher, it'll bounce off the front wall at some point in the neighborhood of center court and set up your opponent for an easy return. Another caution: if you hit the ball on the side wall at a spot too close to your body, then the ball will again never reach the front, and, conversely, if you hit it to a spot too far away from your body, it'll end up in the middle of the front wall.

As you move further towards the back of the court to make your boast, things get tougher. The angles are more acute and the boast becomes defensive. For this shot, turn and face into the back corner. Lead with your right foot. Get well down to the ball. As before, hit with the motion of a backhand drive, but take the racket lower than you normally would for a drive. Remember that you may not have much room to operate in the tight quarters of the corner and keep your stroke accordingly more compact. There's not much room for a grand follow-through. Stay low with your body. Keep your head down and your feet still. And bear in mind that you must lift the ball high on the side wall in order to make sure that it eventually reaches the front (though, as you become more proficient

Mid-court Boast (Backhand)
Hit the ball as you would a
backhand drive but position
yourself so that the ball strikes
the side wall in the backhand
court at an angle, about 45
degrees, that will carry it to its
final destination in the front
corner on the forehand side of
the court. Step forward and
into the side wall, leading with
your right foot, as you make
the shot. Make contact between racket and ball slightly
behind the lead food and drive
and ball firmly into the wall,
following through in the complete way that you would on a
conventional backhand drive.

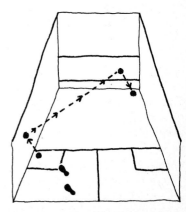

Backhand Mid Court
Boast

Back Court Boast

The ball has bounced deep into the back court, tight to one of the corners, and your job is to boast it to the front corner on the opposite side of the court. Turn your body in a stance that aims the line of your feet towards the corner. Step into the ball — and at the same time into the corner — with your front foot. Don't crowd too close to the corner or you won't have room for a full swing. Stroke the ball with the usual motion of a drive but make contact with the ball at a point slightly in front of the lead foot. Aim at a spot shoulder high on the side wall. You need the height in order to make the ball bounce all the way into the opposite front corner.

with the shot, you can lower your height). The boast, I repeat, is all a matter of angles. From a certain spot on the side wall, given your personal power and talents with a corner boast, the ball will follow a path to the front corner on the opposite side of the court. Find the spot. Find the angle.

This back-court boast, I should add, can become an attacking shot if your opponent doesn't watch the ball or if he's slow on his feet. Suppose he's given to watching the front wall instead of the ball. Well, then you can slip an offensive-style boast past him if you're alert. The same applies if he's too slow at rushing and covering your boast. The shot turns into a real instrument of attack.

The procedures are the same on the forehand boast as on the backhand boast. You strike it as you would a forehand drive with the familiar two exceptions: you're driving the ball into the side wall, not the front wall, and you're making contact with the ball just back of your lead foot (the left in this case), not opposite the lead foot. As to angles, aim and accommodations in the stroke, transpose the tactical points I explained for the backhand boast to the forehand boast. The techniques are the same; so, alas, are the problems.

The Cross Court

You're standing somewhere in the neighborhood of the service box on the forehand side of the court. The ball comes at you, and you hit it with a forehand drive on an angle off the front wall and deep into the backhand court. What you've just executed is a cross-court shot. Or you're standing about mid-court on the backhand side, and when the ball comes at you, you drive it on your backhand off the front wall and deep into the forehand side of the court. That, too, is a cross-court shot.

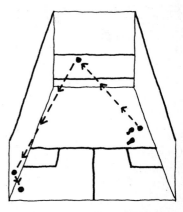

Forehand Cross Court Drive

The main purpose of a cross court is to change the direction of play. Your opponent has got a rally going in a certain direction, and suddenly you spring a cross-court shot and turn the tables on him. Sometimes, for example, I'll hit a cross court off my opponent's boast (though usually you should hit the ball down the wall off a boast).

You don't necessarily have to play a cross-court shot from the front of the court, as I do when I hit it off the boast. You can play it from front court, middle court, back court. The important point, no matter where you hit it from, is to get past your opponent. The ball must go deep. If the opponent is able to chop off your cross court before it gets into the back area, then he'll have a big advantage over you, especially if you've hit the cross-court off a boast and you're still at the front of the court. Again, if you don't hit the cross court deep enough and it lands on the floor around mid-court, then your happy opponent will be blessed with a shot that has winning potential.

How do you hit a proper cross-court shot? First the good news: you hit it, on both a backhand and forehand shot, in the same way that you strike an ordinary backhand or forehand drive. Now the bad news: there are a couple of tricky adjustments that you must make in the ordinary backhand and forehand drive. The spot where you make contact with the ball is different. On the ordinary drive, you meet the ball when it's level with the front foot or very slightly in front of it. With the cross court, you meet the ball well ahead of the front foot, the right foot in the case of the backhand cross court. You follow all the procedures as on the routine drive — same backswing and follow-through, same shifting of weight and positioning of feet — except that you must bang the ball before it reaches a point opposite the front foot.

Another factor that defines the difference between a drive and a cross court is the area on the front wall at which you aim the shot. With the drive, you aim straight ahead. With the cross court, you're playing the old angles game. Let's say that you're operating from a position in the forehand court about one-quarter of the way from the right-hand wall and three-quarters of the way from the left-hand wall. Got that? Well, from that position, you'd aim a cross-court shot at just about center on the front wall. By hitting at the center, your cross court would follow the path that a cross court should follow, which is to say that it would bounce off the front wall, then land low on the side wall behind the service box or on the floor very close to the side wall behind the service box. At both landing points, ideally, the ball would swiftly die. You'd aim the ball at the same target — the center of the front wall — if you were hitting a backhand cross-court shot from a similar position in the backhand court. But as you move away from the specific position I've described — one-quarter of the way from one wall and three-quarters of the way from the other — then you must readjust your target on the front wall. As is so often the case in squash, the spot on the wall becomes a matter of personal judgment. The spot's height on the front wall varies according to the position on the court from which you hit the shot; as you move closer to the front of the court, you aim lower on the front wall. All this, however, must be adjusted depending on your own power.

The Lob

The lob is hit mainly from the front of the court and hit mainly as a defensive shot. You call on the lob, for example, when you're down front and need to buy a bit of time to get back to the center. Hit a lob and you've got the necessary time. That's defensive stroking. The lob can be used as an attacking shot, though, when you're in a position to hit one that will pin your opponent to the back of the court forcing him to boast, which sets up a drop shot on your next turn at the ball. As an offensive shot, the lob must be hit perfectly, deep into the back court, because a weak lob, one that bounces at center court, will be easy for your opponent to return.

On both the forehand and backhand, there are two sorts of lobs. One goes cross court and the other flies down the wall (in effect floating over your head). On the down-the-wall lob, you make contact with the ball ahead of the front foot and away from your body; on the cross-court variety, you make contact further ahead of the front foot and closer to the body.

Now for the actual execution of the shot. Again on both forehand and backhand, you follow the same general principles. Take a moderate backswing, not as far back as for a drive. Step forward and to the side, more towards the front than you would on a drive. Keep the racket face open. Get down to the ball, and on your stroke, hit up and under the ball. That's the key. Come up on the ball from down below, hitting it in front of your front foot and with your weight shifting to that foot (the left on a forehand lob, the right on a backhand lob). Hit the ball firmly; if

Forehand Lob
Keep the racket face open at
all times. That's to guarantee
that you swoop up from under
the ball, which is the secret of
a good lob. You must make the
ball bounce high off the front
wall, and you need a fairly
short backswing, an open
racket face and a stroke that
calls the whole arm into play.
A lob isn't a flick of the wrist;
it's a complete stroke that
finishes with a high follow-
through. Get under the ball
and lift it high on the front
wall.

your strike is too hard, though, it'll bounce off the back wall and permit your opponent an easy return. Hit it high on the front wall, as close to the top red line as possible; if you strike it too low at the front, it'll bounce back to center court and, as before, give your opponent an easy crack at a return.

A word about the follow-through: make it full. A common error is to cut short the follow-through and even to let the wrist slide loose. Keep a firm wrist and follow through in a fairly large arc. Otherwise you'll never get the height on the front wall that's essential to the success of any lob.

For both kinds of lob, cross court and down the wall, remember the path you want the ball to follow. On the cross court, it should hit high on the front wall, float tantalizingly through the air, glance off the side wall at a good height back of the service box, land on the floor close to the back wall, then into the back wall where, if things go perfectly, it'll die before your opponent can get his racket on the ball. On the down-the-wall lob, the ball should hit high on the front wall almost immediately in front of you, brush down the side wall without touching it, bounce to the floor well back of the service box and, to the eternal frustration of your opponent, die on the back wall.

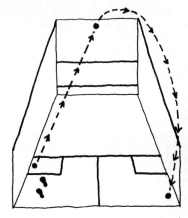

Backhand Cross Court Lob

The Return of Service

It's the second shot hit in any rally and sometimes, especially with beginning players, it's also the last shot. Many beginners flub their return of service and award their opponent a fast and easy point. The problem in almost one hundred per cent of the cases of a failed return is timidity. You should be bold on your return. You should hit it early. Try your best not to let the ball get past you and bound into the back corner. If it does, you'll be forced into playing a strictly defensive return, which will offer your opponent a prime chance for a winner. Avoid those troubles and step bravely into the return at the earliest possible moment.

Let's start with your position as you're waiting for your opponent to serve. Whether you're in the forehand court or the backhand court, stand a foot or two diagonally

Forehand Return of Service

Stand just back of the point of the service box in the forehand court in the ready position. You're facing into the side wall but, glancing over your shoulder, you keep your eyes on the ball as your opponent prepares to knock a lob service in your direction. Do not, above all, concentrate your eyes on the front wall. As the ball bounces toward you, follow the procedures for a forehand volley. Step into the ball with your racket back and wrist cocked. Reach high. Try to make contact with the ball before it strikes the side wall. Volley for length.

Backhand Return of Service
Take up position slightly behind the point of the service box in the backhand court. You're going to return a lob service. Hold your racket in the ready position. As the ball arches toward you from the front wall, take a step forward and sideways in the usual movement for a volley. Reach high for the ball and try to take it before it strikes the side wall. Always keep your eye on the ball — not on the front wall — from the very beginning of your opponent's service. But at the same time you must face into the side wall. In other words, watch your opponent from over your shoulder and simultaneously prepare your body for the step forward into the ball.

behind the corner point of the service box. You're outside the service box, slightly back of it. Your racket is in the ready position, and your body is facing slightly toward the wall on your side of the court. And your eyes? They're on the ball even when it's merely resting in your opponent's hand as he prepares to serve. Many beginners mistakenly watch the front wall rather than the ball, and by doing so, they automatically sacrifice an instant or so of reaction time. If they don't see the ball until it's already coming off the front wall, a couple of milliseconds have been lost during which they might have been preparing to smack a return.

Watching the ball, you see it arch from the front wall, a good lob service or a hard service, and head in your direction. One thought runs through your mind: you're going to hit the ball before it sneaks past you. Whether you catch it on the fly directly from the front wall or whether you take it as it comes off the side wall, you're going to hit a good volley. (If you take it off the side wall, be sure to let it come clear of the wall before you volley. Some players get impatient, hit at the ball too soon and end up cracking the racket on the unyielding wall.) So, as the ball approaches, you have the racket well back, you step forward towards the side wall, reach high and complete the standard volley stroke.

As you make the stroke, you should already have formed an idea about the direction in which you want to send the ball. Don't be too daring in your notions. I'm a conservative in the matter of service return. I don't advocate that you go for anything fancy in the way of an answer to a serve. Try for one of two returns: either a hit that knocks the ball to good length down the wall on your side of the court or a hit that takes the ball cross court to equally good length. You can manage both these returns on a volley off a lob service or a hard service, and in so doing, you'll move your opponent to the back of the court and give yourself plenty of time to set up at center court. That makes good sound tactical sense.

Now if you're confident and skilled and just a little flamboyant, there are three other possible types of return. One is a volley that goes short down the side wall, hits low on the front wall and drops quickly to the floor. The

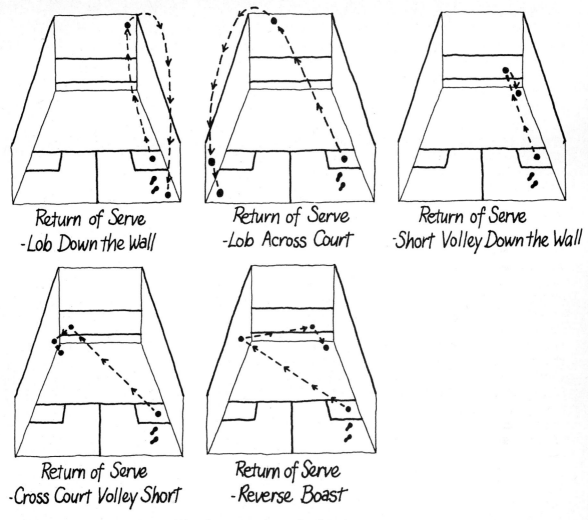

Return of Serve
-Lob Down the Wall

Return of Serve
-Lob Across Court

Return of Serve
-Short Volley Down the Wall

Return of Serve
-Cross Court Volley Short

Return of Serve
-Reverse Boast

second is a cross-court volley that goes into the front corner, front wall to side wall to floor as swift as a wink. The third is a reverse boast which hits the opposite side wall and rebounds into the front wall at a point three-quarters of the way back across to your side of the court. All of these returns are usually good for winners and take the service away from your surprised opponent, but they also have built-in dangers. They are difficult shots, and if you misfire on them, you've lost something precious — a point.

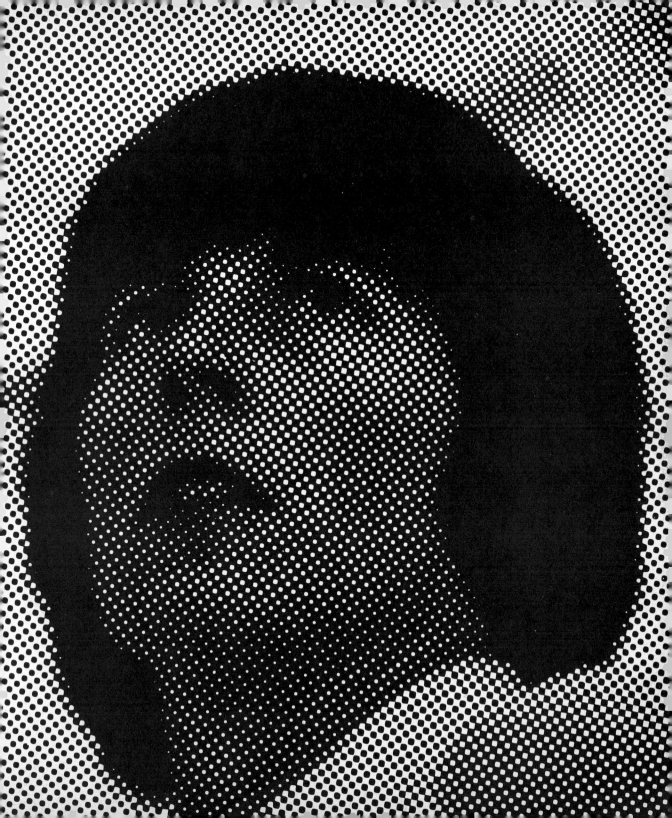

CHAPTER FOUR

Tricks of the Trade: Ten Basic Squash Tactics

In the summer of 1960, just before my first Australian Championships, I had two lessons from Hashim Khan, the first of the world's great squash players. He was touring through Australia, playing exhibitions and offering sessions of coaching, and anyone who cared to could book a lesson from him. When he reached Canberra, I said to myself, hell, why not? I was as nervous as you'd expect any small-town teenager to be, but when I got on court with Hashim, he presented me with my earliest instruction in a very basic tactic: going for winners. In those days, you see, I was a retriever. I kept returning the ball until finally my opponent made an error and gave me a point. That was my style.

No, no, Hashim told me that day in Canberra, don't play the game like that. Go for winners when they come up. Don't wait endlessly for your opponent's errors. Take the initiative. You can't force winners, he said, but as soon as the good shot is there for you, you must seize on it. That was the lesson I took away from Canberra, and though I must admit that even today I'm often too tentative in a game, regressing to my former cautious style, I've never lost sight of the value of Hashim's important advice.

I'm proud to say, too, that Hashim has never quite forgotten me. We met for a second time sixteen years later to play an exhibition match in a town called Markham near Toronto. "I remember you," he said to me. "I remember you from Canberra. Very good player." He

then proceeded to beat me two games to one even though
he was more than a quarter of a century older than I was.
Hashim *always* goes for winners.

Anyway, Hashim Khan's lesson is typical of the sort of
tactical thinking that every squash player should adopt.
The first step in mastering the game is of course to learn
the strokes and to get them in solid working order. Once
that's accomplished, it's time to learn the strategies that
are sure to radically improve the quality of your game.

TEN BASIC SQUASH TACTICS

1. Cultivate the killer instinct. **After the narrow
escape in the match with Anna Craven Smith that I
mentioned earlier in the book, Bob Howe tore a strip off
me. He gave me a lecture that was, to put it mildly, stern.
Bob Howe was a leading Australian tennis player of the
1950s and '60s, and when he saw me against Anna, he
was furious that I'd let her off the hook. He said that, in
any tournament, my job was to walk on the court and get
the match over with, favorably, as quickly as possible.
Never, he said, ease up on an opponent. Not ever. No
matter how far out in front you are, don't slack off your
intention to beat the opposition until the game is safely
tucked away in the win column.**

Bob was right, as I knew only too well. You must
approach each match with a generous supply of killer
instinct tucked in among your talents. Despite my lapse
against Anna, I have plenty of that rare commodity and
use it to maximum effect. The killer instinct is wanting to
win badly enough without becoming unsportsmanlike.
It's realizing that your job is not to give your opponent a
pleasant run around the court. It's feeling the drive to win
— and to win in a hurry. Although not all players are
born with killer instinct, they would do well to cultivate it
as the most essential ingredient, after technical skill, in a
squash victory.

2. Practice deception. **The idea is to fool your
opponent by setting him up for a shot he isn't expecting.
When, for example, you've hit three or four drop shots in**

the course of a game from a spot in front of the serving box on the forehand side of the court, the next time you take a ball in the same spot, your opponent is going to expect you to go for another drop shot. Don't. Hit a lob or go cross court. At the very least, your small piece of deception will place your opponent on the defensive, and at the very best, you'll put a winner across on him.

The ideal situation for deception comes when you find yourself with the clear potential to hit either a drive down the wall or a cross court. Let's say the ball is coming off the front wall to your backhand close to the left side wall. Move yourself into position as if you're going to hit for length. Get right down to the ball. By now, your opponent should be convinced that you've got a drive down the wall in mind. But instead you take the ball a little bit early, make contact out in front of your right foot and hit it cross court to the right front corner. Or, in a variation on that routine, you can give all appearances of going cross court, then hold back on your stroke at the last moment and drive the ball down the wall. In either case, you're certain to throw your opponent off stride.

Remember, though, that successful deception is more likely to belong to the repertoire of the experienced player. As a beginner, concentrate first on learning proper execution of the basic shots before you move into the complicated business of trickery. Remember, too, that the front of the court is the most sensible place to practice deception. After all, the ball has a long way to travel when you hit it from the back of the court, long enough for your intention to be uncovered and foiled by your opponent.

3. Hide the ball. Actually I'm against this notion. Some players rave about the value of putting your body between the ball and your opponent, thereby supposedly screening the opponent's view of the ball until you've hit your shot. Maybe it's a useful gimmick to some players, giving them a small edge over an opponent whose reaction time is slow, but by and large I think it's a dangerous tactic. The problem is that, in moving your body to hide the ball, you're most likely putting yourself out of position to hit the shot from the proper stance.

You're so busy blocking off your opponent's vision that you end up putting the ball into the tin or fluffing an easy return. As far as I'm concerned, hiding the ball is just an unnecessary way of messing up a shot.

You often hear a player say that he can't see the ball on the court. That complaint doesn't mean that the player's opponent has a talent for hiding the ball. It just means that the player has been taking up incorrect positions on the court. Remember always to move so that the ball is in sight at all times.

4. Learn to read a game. In 1971, I was playing a match against Sue Newman in New South Wales. It was the first game, and all of a sudden I found myself down 7-2. What, I thought, is going on here? What was going on, as I quickly realized, was that I was standing there and playing a straight driving game with her, which she, obviously, was winning. That's how I read the game, and I immediately changed tactics. I started to move Sue around, making her run about the court so that she couldn't get set for drives. The change paid off, I won the game 9-7, and went on to take the match.

Reading your opponent is simply a matter of figuring out his strong points and his favorite shots — and then steering him away from them. Reading is a difficult art and comes mainly through experience. It's made even tougher by squash's natural speed. You might successfully read an opponent's style, but by the time you've got it reasoned out, the game could already be out of reach. Still, the idea is never to leave your brains behind when you step on to the court. Look for patterns in your opponent's play. When you hit a boast shot to him, does he invariably reply with a cross-court hit? He does? OK, make sure you're in the right position after each one of your boasts to meet a cross court. Cluing into this type of pattern can turn the tide in your favor and you should train yourself to develop this ability.

Footnote: Try not to let the opponent read *your* game. Vary your shots. Don't repeat familiar patterns. Practice a little deception.

5. *Develop a sense of pace.* If I'm nervous at the beginning of a match — I often am — I don't try anything fancy early in the first game. I keep my shots simple until I feel myself getting well into the game. How do I manage that? Mainly by encouraging long rallies. They work a steadying influence on me and help me to become comfortable with my game and the match. There's nothing worse for your morale than going heavily into battle right off the bat and finding yourself muffing an easy shot and losing a point. To avoid that fate, I pace my way into a game.

For just about the same reasons, I rarely try for a tough service to my opponent at the beginning of a match. I make it a reasonably good serve in terms of length and position, but I never go for the really tricky high-lob service. The reason is that, above all, I don't want to risk a double fault before I've got myself warmed up. A lob serve can easily hit above the line on the side wall for a double fault, and if you blow the service, you find yourself discouraged early with the whole match still stretching in front of you. Play it safe. Pace yourself.

6. *Adjust to physical circumstances.* In the 1960s, the British Championships were always played at the Landsdowne Club right on Berkeley Square in London. The Lansdowne had funny courts, deep in the basement and close to a swimming pool, so close in fact that when you hit a ball hard enough to fly out of the opening at the side of the court, it often bounced through the gallery and ended up floating in the pool. This location meant that the courts were terrifically hot, and the ball bounced around as if it was shot up with pep pills. Under these circumstances, I knew I couldn't play my normal game. I tinkered and fiddled and finally discovered that I got the best control over the ball by slowing down my swing slightly and not hitting with the usual sort of drive.

A little adjustment to your normal style is often necessary, you'll find, on a court that's new and strange to you. Cold court? Hot court? Sweaty plaster walls? Old wood floors that give slower bounces? Check out your surroundings during a warmup, and when something strikes you as just a little offbeat, make adjustments accordingly, particularly in your stroke.

7. Make the right shot. The ball is coming to you deep and about two inches from the side wall. What do you hit? A boast? Don't be silly. You have no room to hit a boast when the ball's right to the wall. Hit a drive.

Too many players go for a shot when the situation is all wrong for that particular shot. They enjoy hitting a boast or a cross court or a lob, so they go for a boast or a cross court or a lob whenever the ball comes in their direction. That's wrong. Practice care. Use some discretion. Only hit a particular shot when it's there, right in front of you, waiting to be hit.

Similarly, if a certain shot isn't working well for you early in a game, don't eliminate it altogether from your repertoire for the rest of the match. That's unnecessarily limiting yourself. Instead, merely cut back on the shot's use until you begin to feel yourself more securely into the game and then gradually bring the shot back into action.

8. Prepare early for your shots. On all strokes, get your racket back and set at the first possible moment. As soon as you know that the ball is coming to your backhand side, take the racket around to your left. Same thing with the forehand, round to the right. Don't be left in a spot where you're forced to hurry a stroke. Early preparation guarantees a better chance at successful execution.

9. Be wise about your movement to the ball. Suppose your opponent has hit a boast from a corner at the back of the court. The ball zips to the opposite corner at the front, striking first the front wall, then the side wall, then the floor. You've been standing at center court and now you're rushing to hit your return. What route do you take to reach the ball? If you travel on a line straight at it, you're making a mistake. Why? Because you'll find yourself too close to the ball and by doing so, you'll have cut down on your selection of shots. A better choice is to move toward the front wall slightly off-center then move toward the ball at the point where it is coming off the side wall. By taking that route, you have three alternatives: you can drive the ball down the side wall, you can go cross court, or you can hit a drop shot. It isn't on every return that you should take the semi-direct path to the ball, but that movement applies to balls hit into the front corners, on both your forehand and backhand sides, and in a more limited way to shots hit off the walls further into the back court. The same applies to balls in the back court. Don't run directly at the ball, but rather follow an indirect route. In squash, there are times when the shortest distance between two points isn't a straight line.

10. Remember the basic purpose in hitting a squash shot. Basically, when you cut out all the frills and theories, what you're trying to do on the court is move your opponent deep with one shot, then take him short with another, and somewhere between the rushing around smack a winner past him or in front of him or around him. Where players go wrong is in not moving the opponent deep enough or short enough. Instead they leave the ball at the center of the court, and it's there, in the neighborhood of the T where the opponent is always going to be lurking, that most games are lost.

Instead, every time you hit the ball you should be trying to make it finish in one of the four corners, where you are most likely to score winners. Remember the killer instinct, and don't make it too easy for your opponent.

Alone on the Court: Practice Drills to Improve your Game

How much information can a person absorb in a forty-minute lesson? Not a bloody lot, especially when the information deals with something as tricky as squash. My solution is make sure that the player goes away with enough in his head to be able to practice correctly the skills I've taught during the lesson.

Practice is the key, and repetition is the key to practice. You may have a terrible boast shot and play a game of squash seven days a week without improving your boast, but you can go on the court and drill yourself in the shot a couple of times a week and almost immediately you'll find your boasts perking up. In this respect, squash is similar to golf. When a pro golfer is hooking his drives, he heads for the practice tee and hits one hundred balls with his driver until he's lost his hook. Squash players who are keen to improve must take a hint from the golfers. Sadly many of them don't, and I find lots of pupils who come back to me for second and third and even fourth lessons and are at the same level of skill as they were when I first saw them. Why? Because they haven't stuck to their practice drills.

For those players who don't mind a little work — and a lot of repetition — there are several recommended drills. They're designed to include practice in all the essential shots in squash, and they fall into two general categories: drills that you work at on your own and drills that you work at in partnership with another player. The first require a certain amount of self-discipline. The second call for plenty of patience and cooperative generosity. Both, provided you perform them in a spirit of rewarding self-improvement, can be enjoyable.

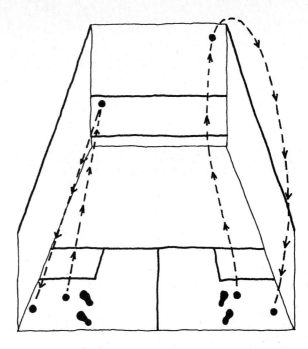

Lob Down the Wall to Length
Drive Down the Wall to Length

SINGLE DRILL 1

This is a drill for forehand and backhand to length. Take up position on the right side of the court close to the wall and back of the service box. Drive the ball up and down the wall on your forehand. That's all. Just drive. Make the ball bounce consistently from the front wall to a point behind the service box. It may sound simple, but it should help you develop an essential game skill. What you're doing is seeking out your spot on the front wall, the spot from which your forehand drive will always come off the front and hit deep enough in the back court to give your opponent trouble. You're discovering through practice the length of your forehand. Try the same drill on the other side of the court to find your spot and your length of the backhand. Again, take on the drill on both sides, forehand and backhand, substituting the lob for the drive. How long should you spend at this drill? At least a few minutes. That's time for a lot of strokes. When you miss a shot, pick up the ball and start again. If your forehand drive seems to be in good order, then concentrate on the backhand drive. Or the forehand lob. Or the backhand lob. Actually, the plan to follow during practice time is to select the drills that emphasize the shots in which you need most work.

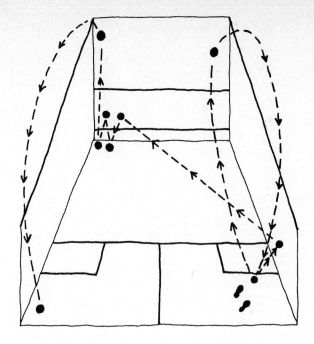

Drop-Boast-Drive

SINGLE DRILL 2

This is a drop-boast-drive drill. Stand at the back of the court on the right side and, to start things off, hit a high soft shot down the right side wall. When the ball reaches you, boast it to the left front corner. Run up and hit a drop shot into the same corner. Then, off the drop, drive the length down the left wall. Run back and boast to the right front corner, and follow the same routine. The order of shots goes like this: boast, drop, drive, boast, drop, drive. All the while you're switching sides with the boasts.

This drill is good for conditioning and good for ball control. But it takes a bit of getting used to. When you first attempt it, you'll have to hit fairly soft shots in order to give yourself enough time to hustle from shot to shot. But as time goes on, as you develop more skills, you can gradually pick up the pace and find yourself rushing about the court at a terrific rate.

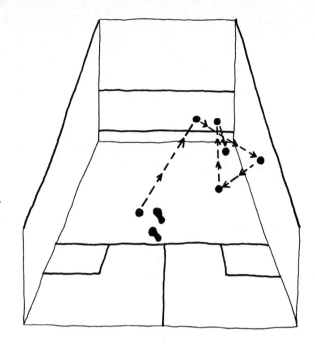

Drop from Mid Court

SINGLE DRILL 3

This is an exclusive drop-shot drill. Stand a few feet in front of the T on the right side of the court. Bounce the ball on the floor to your left on the backhand side. This gets you started. Hit the ball on your backhand into the right front corner, front wall to side wall to floor, so that it lands on your forehand side. Turn your body and hit a forehand drop shot into the same corner.

You see what you're doing here? You're practicing the forehand drop shot, but you're making yourself move to the ball as you might in a game. You're not simply taking up a position for a forehand drop shot and holding on to it. Instead, you're switching your feet and racket into their proper forehand positions while the ball is in the air. You're simulating game conditions.

When the ball comes back after your drop shot, pick it up and start over again. Hit. Hit. Hit. And then switch over to the left side of the court and try the same drill for your backhand drop shot, first setting up the drill with a forehand into the corner from which you'll hit the backhand drop.

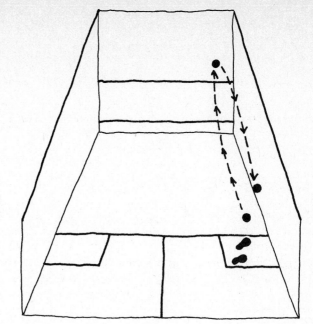

Volley Down the Wall

SINGLE DRILL 4

A volley drill. Stand at the short line close to the right wall. Hit the ball off the front wall back to yourself on the fly and keep on hitting it for as long as you can without the ball bouncing on the floor and without it touching the side wall. The point is to keep the ball in the air with a series of clean and pure volleys. Work on the drill from the forehand side and from the backhand side. This may sound deceptively easy, but it's in fact a challenging, skill-developing exercise.

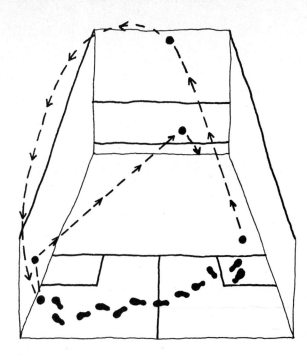

Practice Serve and then Boast Off Serve

SINGLE DRILL 5

Let's not ignore your serve. In effect, this amounts to target practice. You stand in the proper service position, alternating sides of the court, and aim the ball as close to the top red line as you can manage without hitting out. Just keep stroking the ball till you've got at least half-way to perfecting a lob service. It's dull — you have to chase the ball after each serve — but it pays off. Don't, by the way, take three or four balls on court to save yourself time in constantly fetching one lonely ball. The trouble with that plan is that none of the balls will get sufficiently warmed up. You'll find yourself striking the cold balls differently than you would in a regular game with a warmed-up ball.

You can brighten up this drill by running across the court to return your serve with a boast.

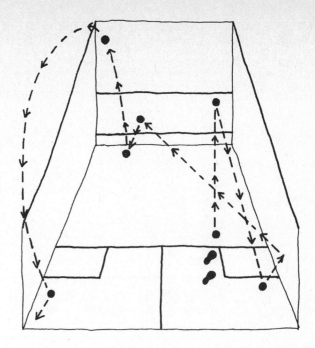

Down the Wall- Boast- Lob - Down the Wall

SINGLE DRILL 6

A boast-lob drill. Stand behind the short line on the forehand side of the court. Hit the ball down the right side wall. When it lands in the back court, boast it to the left front corner. Chase down the boast and play a lob, either cross court or down the left wall. Walk to the back of the court. Pick up the ball. Start over again. The idea of this drill is to make yourself run hard for the ball from back court to front court. I mean *really* hard. Be sure, too, that you take turns alternating the lobs, first cross court, then down the wall, and so on. You need facility in both.

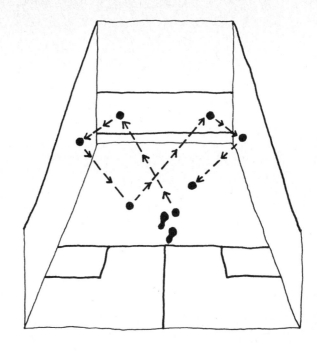

A Control Drill

SINGLE DRILL 7

A control drill. This is one of the most difficult of single drills. Stand in the middle of the court. Stroke the ball on your forehand so that it hits low on the front corner, front wall, side wall, and back to you at center court. When it returns, without pausing, hit the ball on your backhand into the opposite front corner. Then, as it returns, forehand into the first corner, backhand, forehand and on and on. Keep the ball moving in a rhythm. The first time I tried this drill, years ago, I could only bang it three or four times in a row. Gradually I caught the knack of it, and the most I've hit without a break is just over ninety. The drill leaves your arm absolutely limp from the effort, but it works wonders for your control of the ball and makes you conscious of your footwork.

So much for the single drills. Actually the short list I've given you doesn't by any means exhaust all the possibilities. If you have an inventive turn of mind, it's not difficult to improvise your own drills. The important point is to emphasize shots that you'll use in a real game. Don't, for example, concoct a drill that gives you five minutes of practice on mid-court shots. It'll be a bad game in which you find yourself playing shots like that. Be realistic, but try to give yourself a hard workout.

The same advice applies to double drills for two players. They're more demanding, indeed especially difficult for beginners. Each player in a double drill must maintain a delicate balance between competition and team work. Each would like to beat the other player, but each would equally like to keep the drill going. Use a sensible division of both impulses in performing the drill. It's no use to have one player smashing the ball past his partner when a drill has only just begun. In a doubles drill, don't look for winners; look for practice.

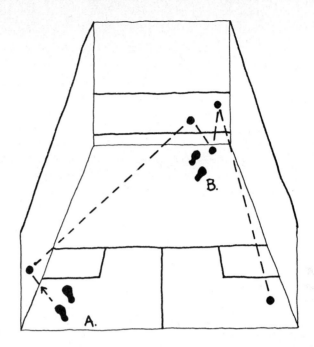

"A" Boasts- "B" Lobs or Drives Down the Wall

DOUBLE DRILL 1

Player *A* stands in the left back corner. Player *B* takes up position at center court. *A* boasts to the right front corner. *B* runs to the corner and drives or lobs down the right side wall. *A* moves across the back court and boasts from the right back corner. *B* lobs or drives off the boast down the left wall. *A* boasts again. *B* drives or lobs and round and round they go. *B*, the player at the front, decides whether to drive or lob depending on his relation to the ball on each shot. If he has good position on the ball, then he drives. If his position is poor, he settles for a lob. In either event, as he switches from side to side, he's getting practice on both forehand and backhand, and the same goes for *A*, who is boasting off his forehand and backhand. What next? Well, naturally after a bit, *A* and *B* change positions and run through the drill again. In most double drills, players should alternate positions.

To add an extra dose of difficulty to the drill, *A* and *B* can also be required to move to the T between shots. That is, after a player has boasted from the left back corner, he must get to the T before he heads to the right back corner for his next boast. This will give his legs solid conditioning.

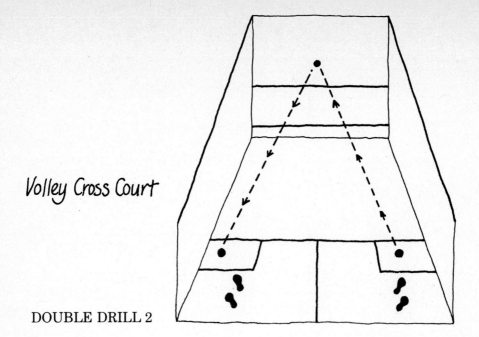

Volley Cross Court

DOUBLE DRILL 2

A and *B* start off at opposite sides of center court, each out from a wall. *A* volleys the ball to *B*. *B* returns the volley. Back and forth goes the ball, each shot a volley. At first, the two players content themselves with routine and easy-to-return hits, but as they get into the drill, they begin to add some testing twists to the action. *A*, for example, hits his volleys as close to *B*'s side wall as possible in order to make *B* watch both the ball and the wall. *B*, for his part, hits one volley high and deep and the next lower and much harder, thereby moving *A* up and down the court to make his volley returns. And so it goes, a contest of both players' strokes, eyes and finesse with the volley.

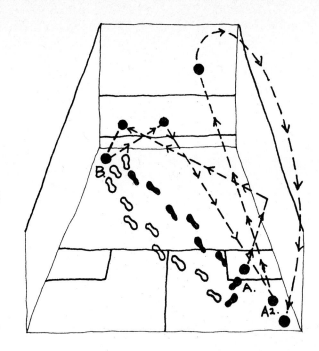

Boast-Cross Court-Down the Wall

DOUBLE DRILL 3

Here's a drill that runs in a circular pattern, taking each player in turn through three different shots. It begins with *A* in a back corner and *B* in front of the T. *A* boasts. *B* plays a cross-court shot off of *A*'s boast. The ball returns to *A* at the back of the court and he drives or lobs the ball to length. *B*, in the meantime, has returned to the T, then moved to the back corner and hits a boast, which *A*, who has come down to the front after he hit his drive, promptly plays a cross-court shot. *B*, ready and waiting at the T, takes his turn at a drive for length, just in time for *A* to return a boast. And off they go again in the same intricate series of shot switches until both *A* and *B* collapse in a pool of perspiration.

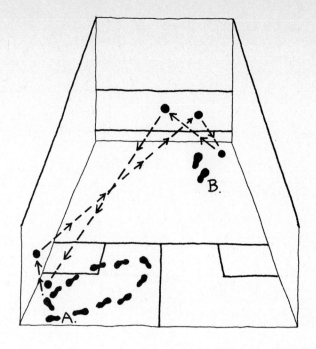

"A" Boasts "B" Drives
Cross Court

DOUBLE DRILL 4

A is in his familiar spot in one of the back corners. *B* is in the front court. *A* boasts. *B* hits either a cross-court lob or a cross-court drive, depending on the position he's able to get on the ball, that takes the ball straight back to *A*'s corner. *A* hits another boasts and *B* once again replies with a cross-court shot, either lob or drive. And so on. It sounds like an easy drill for *A*, but it's not. What's the catch? After each boast, *A* must desert his corner, run to the T and make it back to the corner in time for his next boast. That's strenuous. *A* can work this drill from both corners of the back court and then switch places with *B* to let him have a taste of boasting between trips to the T.

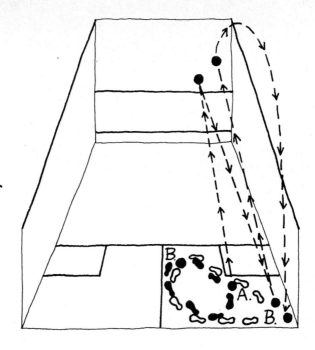

Clearing the Back Corner

DOUBLE DRILL 5

A, standing at the back of the court on his forehand side, drives a ball down the wall trying for good length. After he has made his stroke, he moves briskly out of the corner and allows *B*, who has been standing a couple of feet behind the T, to move into *A*'s original position and to have his own turn at a drive down the wall. *A*, meanwhile, has looped around to *B*'s starting spot, and as soon as *B* has completed his drive, *A* moves back for a second drive while *B* backs out. It's like a ballet with both players moving in and out of the corner in a circular path and taking turns at the ball. It's also a perfect drill for learning to clear a corner. The point is that if you don't know how to clear properly in a game, you might run into your opponent, have a let called against you and lose the benefits of a good shot. The same drill applies to lobs as well as drives and should be practiced on both forehand and backhand sides of the court.

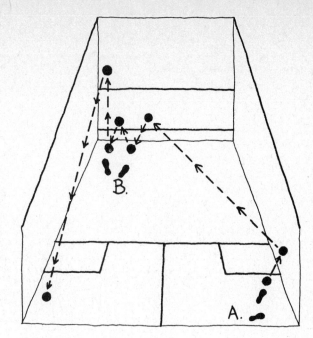

"A" Boasts - "B" Drops and then Hits His Own Drop Down the Wall

DOUBLE DRILL 6

This is a drop-shot drill for two players. *A* boasts from the back court on his forehand side. *B*, at the front of the court, hits a drop shot off the boast and then — surprise — *B* returns his own drop shot with a drive down the side wall. *A*, who has in the meantime taken a trip to the T and back, smacks another boast, which gives *B* a chance to repeat his double-shot routine, drop and drive, on the opposite side of the court. After a couple of minutes, the two players switch positions and charge through the drill all over again.

CHAPTER SIX

Safety on the Court

"Oh my god," I thought when the ball hit me on the side of the eye, "there it goes! There goes the chance of my life!"

This incident occurred in the semi-finals of the first Women's World Open Squash Championship in Brisbane in August 1976, the tournament that I trained harder for than any other in my whole career. I'd been considered the best in the world for years, but until that tournament was finally organized, there had been nothing that officially confirmed me as the world's champion. What hurt almost as much as the injury was that I couldn't blame anybody except myself. I'd played a stupid shot in a match against Margaret Zachariah, an excellent player from Australia. A shot of hers had taken me to the front of the court where I should have driven the ball to good length to allow myself time to get back in position. Instead, hitting on my forehand, I played a poor half-court shot that didn't give me any chance to get out of the road of her return. She came across court with her shot and caught me moving crabwise. I was taking a quick peek behind me to see what Margaret was doing, and — *wham* — the ball rocketed into the corner of my right eye.

The referee stopped play to allow me a chance to recover, and I started to walk around the court, tears streaming out of my right eye. I didn't want to step off the court because if I did, the referee might rule a default in Margaret's favor. In the first minute or so of walking around, I wasn't sure I'd ever recover. Fortunately my eyesight gradually began to return, and I could see at least well enough to take up play again to win the match.

The point I want to make with this story isn't that squash is a dangerous game, as risky as ice hockey or football, but that, on the contrary, provided you follow sensible precautions, it's as safe as a stroll on the beach. The fact is that the better you become at squash, the less likely you are to run into injuries. Good players don't hit and bang one another. With poor, careless players the story can be different. Almost all the horrendous accidents, the ones that frighten potential players away from squash, happen in the lower grades among players without the training or the sense to take care of themselves and their opponents. If a player, either beginner or veteran, follows certain basic safety rules, then the chances of receiving or causing an injury can be reduced to the barest minimum. In my own experience, I have been involved in only four minor injuries in several thousand games.

EIGHT KEY SAFETY RULES

1. Watch the ball. That sounds simple, so simple that some players might wonder why I mention it. Unfortunately, what happens all too often is that a player watches the front wall instead of the ball. He makes his shot, hitting the ball deep, then moves to the T with his opponent behind him and concentrates his attention on the front wall waiting for the opponent's hit. A fraction of a second later, he grows impatient and begins to wonder where the devil the ball has got to. He turns his head to look and — *bam* — he catches his opponent's return in the face. This type of accident can be avoided if the player keeps his eye constantly on the ball, so that there is time, room and opportunity to clear out of the way of an oncoming ball.

2. Don't crowd an opponent. Crowding usually results from anxiety. Player *A* hits a poor shot. He realizes the odds are high that Player *B,* his opponent, is going to return a winner. *A* grows anxious. He's eager to have a try at *B*'s return. Too eager. He moves close to *B* in an effort to improve his chances of retrieving *B*'s shot. Too close. *B*'s swing comes around in its natural arc and his racket clips *A* in some vulnerable part of the anatomy. *A*'s not only lost his chance to return the ball but also probably a little blood.

3. Remember the rule about lets. It reads, in part, as follows: "A let may be allowed if the player refrains from hitting the ball owing to a reasonable fear of injuring his opponent." In other words, if an opponent is unavoidably in the path of your shot, don't try to hit around him. Stop immediately. Call for a let. Avoid possible bloodshed. Above all, don't barge into him in a desparate bid to play a winner. The rules in a situation like that "let" you off the hook. Take advantage of them.

4. Be flexible in your court strategy. Many beginners, for example, are told that, after they hit the ball, they should hurry to position themselves at the T. OK, they think, if that's how you're supposed to play the game, then they'll head for the T come hell or high water. It doesn't matter where the ball happens to be on the court, they home in on the T. This can be a foolish error. As a general rule, it's a good idea to take up a stance just behind the T, but for safety's sake, it's more important to check out the whereabouts of the ball before making a move. A beginner who's too intent on the T is sooner or later going to take a thump from a flying ball or a swinging racket.

5. Avoid overswinging and opponents who overswing. There's no need in squash to develop an exaggerated backswing and follow-through, and if you find yourself developing this tendency, curb it. You're too likely to clobber another player. As for an overswinging opponent, be careful to give him a wide berth on the court. Either that or find another less lethal opponent.

6. If in doubt, wear eye goggles. This is advice for people who dn't necessarily need glasses but who fear injury to their eyes. The goggles are reasonably priced, made of hard plastic and constructed with slits too narrow to permit a squash ball to make contact with the eye. Players who need glasses could wear one of two pieces of equipment: wrap-around guards over their spectacles or glasses with toughened lenses or soft frames and pop-out lenses that fly harmlessly apart when something strikes them. Unprotected eyeglasses must *not* be worn on the court, as the risk of their shattering and a fragment piercing the eye is a serious one.

7. Consider a mouthguard. After the eyes, the teeth are the part of the body most open to injury. A gaping space where your teeth used to be is too high a price to pay for a game of squash. A mouthguard is a tidy, comfortably fitting, inexpensive apparatus made out of clear plastic and is a worthwhile precaution.

8. Wear two pairs of socks. I'm serious. Blisters are a squash player's persistent enemy, especially for players who spend a lot of time on a hot court. The double thickness cushions the feet, soaks up perspiration, holds the feet firmly in place, and helps prevent blisters. I've never had trouble with my feet, and I attribute a lot of that good fortune to my father who was a fanatic about proper foot care. From the time I started playing tennis, always on hard courts and sometimes in 85-degree heat, my dad made me soak my feet in mentholated spirits when a tournament was approaching. The treatment toughened up my feet, which are still benefiting from dad's advice.

By following these eight simple safety rules on the court, you should be able to escape all but the most unpredictable of accidents. Although squash isn't by any means a "danger" sport, the conscientious player learns to escape injury by exercising consideration and common-sense at all times.

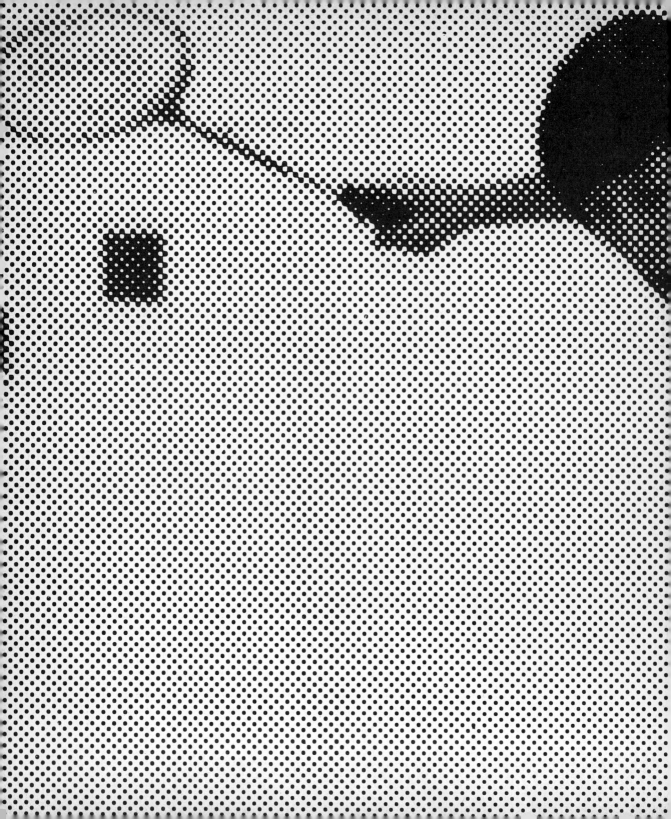

CHAPTER SEVEN

Getting Fit and Staying Fit

Fitness has come increasingly under scientific scrutiny in the last few years, especially in North America. But for most ordinary people — for you, me and the bloke who jogs around the block every morning — it still involves a hit-and-miss struggle to develop a personal fitness program. I'd like to give you some hints from my own experience that I hope will help you to map out a fitness routine that suits your lifestyle and tastes.

Skipping. I tried skipping first when I was a teenager preparing for the Australian Championships. My father preached skipping because he'd used it successfully in his football-training days. He had a talent for all sorts of tricky skip steps, but I was a straight plugger, skipping rope one thousand steps in the morning and another one thousands at night. This increased my leg strength and improve my cardiovascular system. Later, when I moved to Sydney, a fellow who had made an informal study of fitness pointed out that I'd derive a greater benefit if, instead of skipping the rope for a straight twenty minutes, I skipped extra fast for one minute, then switched for a couple of minutes to calisthenics and then returned to speed skipping, and so on in alternating fashion. I tried his system and he turned out to be right. The advantages of skipping are tremendous. Skipping gets you up on your toes and the balls of your feet, makes you feel light and springy, teaches your feet to move in quick and darting motions. These are essential skills for

125

squash which, of all sports, demands feet that are light, quick, supple, flexible and as springy as a brand new mattress.

Running. I'd always been a runner during my field-hockey years, but it wasn't until I became a regular in squash competition that I approached it as a determined and daily part of a training program. At the beginning, I used to jog down to Cooper Park near my flat in Sydney and run for two miles. Then I'd tackle the steps, eighty of them, that led out of the park. I'd run up them as fast as I could manage, then back down, then up again. The effort bloody near killed me, but it kept me in great shape, and running has remained a constant part of my training program throughout my career. Five mornings a week I hit the trail and cover two miles, running as fast as I can. It has helped me gain stamina, so that I rarely run out of wind on the court.

Wind-sprints. In addition to stamina, mobility is vital in squash. I've come across lots of squash players who are splendid runners off the court, strong and fast, but who are flops at moving on the court. They stand flat-footed and don't have the necessary quickness off the mark. Practicing wind-sprint drills gives you this kind of mobility.

Mark off ten-yard lengths on a football field or in a park or along a quiet street (actually, lamppost to lamppost will serve the purpose on an ordinary street). Jog for the first ten yards, accelerate into an all-out dash for the next ten, jog the following ten, bust out on the ten after that, and so on, until you've done a couple of hundred yards. Then rest a minute or two and try a second session.

There's a variation on the wind-sprint drill that I often include in my program when I plunge into heavy training for an important tournament. I stand at the back of the squash court and run like hell for the front wall, taking big strides so that I cover as much court as possible in as few strides as possible. I arrange my steps in a way that means my left foot will take the last step as it would if I were moving to the front to play a forehand. (Alternatively, I'll stop on my right foot as I would in playing a backhand.) Then I gently touch the wall and turn around for a similar run to the back. I repeat the dash ten times back and forth, and after each group of ten, I do some stretching exercises or situps. I tackle the same drill running backwards (with exercises in between) and, yet again, the same drill moving sideways and doing cross-over steps (plus the exercises). It's great for all-round fitness and for movement on the court.

Weight-training. Squash isn't a sport that needs bulging muscles, and there's no call for a player to aspire to a Charles Atlas physique. In fact, it would be a drawback in squash to develop cumbersome biceps and rippling chest muscles. But, as I learned in Sydney from a gym instructor, some work with light weights that emphasizes quick repetitions can give you an extra flexible strength.

Be cautious, though, in lifting weights. Don't fiddle with the heavy barbells, and if you insist on developing a weights routine, seek out a qualified instructor who understands squash. Some weight-lifting exercises can be detrimental to the muscles needed by the squash player.

Stretching. Exercises that stretch the leg muscles and loosen up the hamstrings are ideal for squash. Supple and strong legs, which stretching exercises promote, are invaluable in helping a player to recover position after getting down a low shot on the court. I've played against many women who were very quick at getting down to the ball for a shot but who were not nearly so quick at straightening up in preparation for the next shot. Stretching exercises, I'm happy to say, provide the solution.

Stationary bicycling. I tried it first during the months before the Women's World Championship, using two techniques. One was pumping for a short period, about a minute, at a high work load and at a fast speed, and the other was pumping for longer periods, up to five

minutes at high speeds against a lighter work load.
Steady rhythmic pedaling is strenuous exercise and
increased leg fitness will inevitably result from a regular
cycling routine.

DEVELOPING A SAFE PROGRAM

Before you get into a program of fitness, choosing from
the above and other activities, let me offer four safety
precautions:
1. If you haven't been playing any sports for a few years
or are in poor shape or are over, say, thirty-five, get your
doctor to give you a thorough checkup before taking on a
program.
2. Use a variety of activities in your program. More
people are discouraged from exercise by sheer boredom
than by any other cause.
3. Warm up your body before each session with something easy. A light jog, some situps, a little stretching and
rolling of the arms and trunk. Don't go in cold.
4. Stick to it and be regular. A program of about thirty
minutes' duration carried out at least three or four times a
week is a worthwhile target.
  When you're developing your program, pay attention to
the five conditioning areas, which I list below. It's helpful
to take your workouts in a gymnasium or a well-equipped
fitness club where there are instructors available for
consultation and a variety of equipment for several types
of exercise. If such facilities are unavailable, you can
easily construct your own program to carry out at home
or in a local park.

1. Short-duration, high-intensity training. This
includes wind sprints; bicycling at high work loads for
periods of thirty seconds or a minute with ease-ups and
repetitions; circuits of exercises (leg lunges, hurdle jumps,
box steps) which you do in quick succession, stepping up
the number of times you perform each exercise and the
number of times you perform them in succession as your
training progresses.

2. Endurance work. Biking at lower resistance for periods of up to four or five minutes with repetitions. Running long distances.

3. Muscular strength. This, as I said earlier, is a fairly low-priority requirement in squash since it's a sport that calls more for speed and endurance than muscle strength. Still, working with low weights (bars and bells of from ten to twenty pounds) in a high-repetition system (repeating a lifting exercise about twenty times) can provide you with extra strength and tone if you need it.

4. Flexibility. Here's where the stretching exercises come in, especially exercises that emphasize the legs, arms and trunk. Do each of these slowly — don't strain or you'll find yourself pulling a ligament — and stretch as far as your joints, ligaments and tendons will safely permit. You can include such things as the all-over stretch, high leg stretches, semi-splits, the roll up and tuck and a wide variety of similar exercises.

5. Agility. Concentrate on your footwork. Buy a skipping rope and do a minute of fast skipping. Then turn to a stretching exercise. Back to the rope for another fast minute. More stretching. And so on till you've covered four or five minutes with the rope. You'll turn into a squash twinkle-toes in no time.

SQUASH VIS-A-VIS OTHER SPORTS

Based on my own experience, I recommend that every squash player participate in another sport as a complement to squash. I have been playing field hockey since I was thirteen and to this day I find that it rounds out my squash program. The appeal of hockey, oddly enough, is that it is quite opposite to squash in several respects. Hockey is played outdoors, squash indoors. Squash is an individual sport, hockey's a team sport and you play, not for yourself, but as one in a group of eleven. In hockey, you score goals, in squash it's points. In hockey you move around a large, open space while in squash you're confined to a small enclosed court. The change of pace and contrast mean that when I return to the court from the hockey field I go at squash with a fresh new zip.

There are more hockey benefits I could mention, benefits that arise from the similarities between it and squash. Running is one. All that pounding up and down the hockey field keeps my legs and lungs in sound working order for the squash court. Less obvious perhaps is the eye-to-ball coordination that's common to both games. Each sport teaches you to keep your eye on the ball and to handle it with dexterity.

There are any number of sports that make a nice complement to squash and I won't presume to recommend one at the expense of others. Almost all bring pleasure and friendships, not to mention good conditioning. I will say, though, that you can't combine two sports, squash and something else, and expect to play at the top level in both. At least that was my experience when I was a keen tennis player as a youngster. When squash came into my life, I found that I had to give up dreams of glory in tennis. I'm glad I did.

THE WARMUP

Never go on a squash court without first loosening your body. Arriving at a game cold is an invitation to injury, particularly tears and pulls of the muscles and tendons. Devote about five minutes to warmup exercises and take to the court within five minutes of completing the routine. There's not much sense in warming up and then sitting around for half an hour. Here's the warmup routine I recommend.

1. All-over stretch or seals and camels. Lie on your stomach, hands and feet on floor and head up, push your middle into the floor, then raise it high until, if possible, your heels are actually touching the floor at the back. Perform this exercise slowly. Stretch, don't strain. Repeat five or six times.

2. Lateral groin stretch. Stand with your legs fairly wide apart, assume a semi-crouch position and rotate from side to side, working the upper part of the right leg, then the left leg, until you've covered both five or six times.

3. Roll up and tuck. Lie on your back. Raise your body from the waist at the same time tucking up your legs at the knees. Wrap your hands around your knees. Lie down. Start over. Repeat the exercise five or six times.

4. Leg lunges. Reach your right leg out in front of you from a standing start. Squat and clasp the right thigh with both hands, stretching the legs slowly apart. Do the same maneuver with the left leg out front, three times with each leg.

5. Straight and bent arm swing back. Just an easy swinging motion with the arms bent, then extended. Carried on for thirty seconds or so, this will allow your legs to recover, warm the arms gently and get you all set to take to the squash court.

THE WARMDOWN

When you've finished a tough game of squash, your body temperature is likely to be way up. Give it a chance to come back down to normal before you rush off for a shower and change, and return to office or home. Walk up and down the court for two or three minutes after a game or, if somebody's pounding on the court door for their turn at a match stroll in the hall outside. As soon as the body's had long enough to cool, take a leisurely shower. There should be a gradual transition from the speedy action of the court to a normal pace. After a particularly rough match, you might want to drink something with a dash of salt in it, like Gatorade or Staminade.

HEALTHFUL HINTS FOR SQUASH PLAYERS

Physical fitness requires more than just exercise and training. What you put into your body has a great impact on what you get out of it in terms of athletic performance. Although frankness makes me confess that I too often ignore the best advice on diet, liquor and smoking, I want you, the aspiring squash player, to have the benefit of the sensible guidelines endorsed by most sports professionals.

Smoking. I got the habit — or the habit got me — when I was twenty years old, and I didn't shake it until five years later. To tell the truth, at first I didn't notice that the twenty cigarettes a day had any effect on my squash game. Probably I was too young and fit from my training program for smoking to have a noticeable impact on my performance. Even after I developed a smoker's cough, I kept on at my bad habit. It was only after I had quit, cold turkey, that I noticed the difference. I found myself running around the court with more ease. The point is, as I later learned, that a heavy smoker has to work about three times as hard as a nonsmoker. It's carbon monoxide that does the damage. When a smoker takes a puff, he takes in particles of carbon monoxide which push aside the oxygen from the hemoglobin in the red blood cells and leave a deficiency of oxygen in the circulatory system. And it's oxygen, of course, that fuels the body. Over the long haul, a smoker's lungs become clogged with residue, lowering his oxygen intake and making his circulatory system a lot less efficient. I can just imagine myself, if I'd kept at my Craven As, running out of steam in a tough match and never coming close to all the records that I'm proud of today. It wouldn't have been worth it, not for a few puffs of smoke.

The best rule for all squash players, beginners and veterans, pros and amateurs, champions and bottom-of-the-ladder players, is never to pick up the first cigarette. And if it's too late for that, then then second-best rule is to stub out the last cigarette.

Drinking. More athletes than I can count like their drop of alcohol. Australian athletes give the beer companies around the world plenty of business, and I remember hearing that Frank Shorter, the great American long-distance runner, spent the night before his 1972 Olympic Marathon victory relaxing over a drink or two with his wife. Like Frank, I enjoy my Bacardi and Coke or my gin and tonic before dinner and on convivial occasions. However, I think that for anyone who wants to develop into a half-way decent squash player, there are all sorts of reasons for not overdoing it in the liquor department. Alcohol is high in empty calories which contain no nutrition. Alcohol also prevents absorption of several B vitamins, and once alcohol enters the bloodstream, it can slow down the flow of oxygen to the heart and other muscles. The result is to reduce speed and energy on the squash court. It's obvious that liquor sabotages all-round squash performance.

Food. In the area of diet, the usual principles of well-balanced eating apply equall to squash as to other physical activities. When I'm preparing for a tournament I try to follow one simple rule: eat meals that represent a sensible proportion of carbohydrates, fats, proteins and vitamins, and steer clear of fad diets.

A good-sized breakfast, a nutritious lunch of whole-wheat sandwiches and fruit, and a dinner of meat and vegetables comprise my daily regimen. During a tournament I switch over to a high-carbohydrate diet of nuts, spaghetti, cake, ice cream, and other glycogen-producing foods. Current thinking in sports circles is that this diet creates stores of energy that the athlete can draw on in an emergency. Personally, I can't say whether this is true or not, but I can testify that during the 1976 World Championships in Brisbane I felt in tip-top shape on this diet. I would not, however, recommend the high-carbohydrate regimen to non-professional athletes, as it is not a well-balanced diet and could result in nutritional deficiencies and weight problems.

There are two matters concerning eating habits as they relate to squash that I can be more definite about. One has to do with dieting to lose weight, and the other with eating before a game. I've had experiences, sometimes painful, with each.

The rule about food before playing squash is simple: wait at least four hours after a big meal. The results if you don't follow the rule are also simple: cramps. Your stomach isn't designed to accommodate a heavy meal followed by a lot of vigorous exercise. In the years when Brian and I were touring through Australian towns putting on squash exhibitions, the local officials at each stop were always arranging dinners and celebrations of welcome. It was very generous of them, but unfortunately the dinners were invariably scheduled for an hour or less before we were to go on the court. It sometimes got very tricky. I'd try to get by with a bit of fish or some salad, anything light on the digestion, but whatever precautions we took there were still times when we would have to push ourselves back from the table and go straight on the court for a game against one of the local players. I'll never know how we survived.

I have a tendency to put on weight when I'm not in strict training; so, when my weight climbs too high, I become concerned. Once, in 1964, I put myself on a strict diet; for one week, I ate nothing except grapefruit, eggs, spinach and black coffee. I lost four pounds in seven days, and on the seventh, a Sunday I remember, I went out on the squash court with Brian and played a good hard game. Or at least I *tried* to play a good hard game. But I couldn't. The meager diet couldn't sustain me on the court and I felt weak, faint and helpless. That experience taught me an obvious lesson: never combine dieting with strenuous squash. Give up one or the other. If you're going to diet, avoid hard squash games. And if you're going to stick to hard squash, don't put yourself on a debilitating diet.

Here's another piece of advice if you're worried about weight: eat yogurt. I got on to it years ago during one of those periods when I was keeping an eye on my extra four or five pounds, and I still enjoy it a few times every week. I don't necessarily eat yogurt for weight-control reasons (some of the more recent commercial brands, as far as that goes, are actually said to be fattening), but for other beneficial health reasons. Yogurt is an excellent digestive aid and with honey and lemon added it tastes good too.

CHAPTER EIGHT # The Future

I had a taste of the spirit of squash the very first time I stepped on a court, even before I began to play at Leo Casey's courts in Queanbeyan. This happened during a holiday that I took to Sydney with my sister and a girlfriend in the winter (warm-weather time in Australia) when I was seventeen. We spent a day on the beach, walking around without shoes until our feet were black, and then we wandered over to a commercial squash court, pay as you play, in Manley District Park. We thought we'd try a hit. Not with those dirty feet on my clean courts, said the woman running the place. She sent us off to buy some socks. We played in the socks and shoes the woman rented us, and later she took the time to show me the serve and some fundamentals of the game. That free lesson was my first exposure to squash, and that woman was Jean Walker, who later became the president of the Women's Squash Rackets Association in Australia and had much to do with pushing along my career. What was her motive for encouraging me on that first day? Did she recognize a future world champion in the making? Of course not. She was merely offering a bit of generosity, and that's typical in the squash world.

So many people have been kind to me at various times during my career. There was Nell McGrath, who managed Leo Casey's courts and was forever allowing me extras in playing time. There were all the people of Queanbeyan who raised 231 pounds to help pay my way to the first British tournaments in 1962. And there was

Janet Morgan who met me at the airport when I climbed off the place, shy and bloody near tongue-tied, on that first English trip.

Janet Morgan (now Janet Morgan Shardlow) is a remarkable story all by herself. She had been England's greatest woman squash player, winner of the British Championship for ten consecutive years. She had retired from tournament play a couple of years before 1962, and she came to gather me up at the airport and take me under her wing as a veteran champion showing kindness to someone new and nervous at the game. She invited me to live at her home in Surrey, she arranged practice matches with good men players in the area, and she saw me off on planes and trains that took me to the Scottish Championship and the British Championship and all the other tournaments I played throughout Britain. That was the woman whose record of ten straight British titles, considered unbeatable by many people, I was finally lucky enough to top in 1972 when I won over Kathy Malan of South Africa for my eleventh British in a row. The win is still one of my proud favorites, but the irony is that I would never have achieved it, probably never have even approached the record, if Janet hadn't given me such a boost on my first trip to England and, for that matter, on all the rest of my British trips.

It's the Janet Morgan spirit that's going to be especially needed in squash over the next few years, which are bound to be the most significant for the sport in its entire history. In the old days, as recently as the late 1960s, squash was an underdog game. It took second place to the more glamorous individual sports like tennis and golf, the ones that got the television exposure and earned the millions in prize money for the players. Squash was the sport that had to go begging, and it was largely for this reason that it developed among its officials and players and fans the unique sense of generous cooperation. But since the early 1970s, squash's status has been changing. It's beginning to boom all over the world, and some observers feel that it stands in approximately the same position that tennis had reached in the mid-1960s, on the verge of an explosion in popularity. If that's true, if the big bang is about to go off for squash, then it'll need plenty of its old-time spirit to negotiate the enormous changes that lie ahead.

SQUASH'S GROWING POPULARITY

I've come across signs all over the world of a mushrooming interest in squash. Britain today boasts almost 400,000 active squash players, double the number who were in the game when I first started competing in British tournaments. In Canada, the current figure has leaped to 60,000 players, triple what it was a mere five years ago. Toronto ranks as the country's squash headquarters with over three hundred courts, most of them built since 1970. Canadian universities have caught on to squash, and new high-rise apartment complexes across the country can no longer attract young tenants unless they include a squash court or two or three. I've seen similar indications of bubbling enthusiasm in places as varied as Hong Kong and Singapore, Stockholm and Copenhagen and Hamburg, not to forget all of South Africa, which qualifies as a great squash country.

But, of all countries, the wave of the squash future is most accurately signalled in Australia. It's the land that has all along been showing the way with its commercial courts and its encouragement of youngsters to get into the game, two trends that are essential to squash's continued prosperity. In Canada, the sport is at present too confined to private clubs, and most young people don't discover squash until they reach university. While that's true to a lesser degree in England and other countries — Britain is hurrying ahead with pay-as-you-play clubs and with junior programs — it's only in Australia that a couple of fourteen-year-olds can stroll into a commercial squash center, put down their dollar and bag away on a court for at least an hour or more. That's not only sports democracy in action — that's the way to provide a strong basis to the already blossoming popularity of the game.

Why is squash acquiring favor among so many people around the world? That's easy. More than any other sport, it fits into today's atmosphere of hurry-up-and-get-fit. It's a quick game, far less time-consuming than golf, much swifter than tennis. A businessman can easily manage a brisk forty-minute game during his lunch hour. A housewife can arrange a short trip to the courts while the kids are in school. Both will return to their regular duties feeling fit without valuable time missed from office and home. A good squash game is a great relaxant at any time of the day. For all of these reasons, squash qualifies as the "now" sport.

PROMOTING SQUASH

To spread this message to the sporting public, to keep the boom exploding, squash must reach out in one other specific way — through its best players. As my friend Rex Bellamy, the rackets correspondent for the *Times* of London, put is, squash has got to "advertise its best goods in the shop window." The great squash champions must appeal to a wider audience and impress themselves on the average sport fan's consciousness the way the great tennis stars have done through the 1970s. That can be managed, it seems to me, in three ways: by putting squash on television, by building larger spectator galleries for squash championships and by developing a circuit of squash tournaments along the lines of the tennis and golf pro tours.

Squash is a natural for TV with its visually appealing non-stop action. Still, squash presents problems for television and its audience. Seeing the ball is one. Too often, the small black squash ball gets lost on the screen, and the players look to viewers like a couple of people swatting flies. Australian and British TV have been working on solutions and both countries have successfully shown exciting matches. More experimenting, though, is obviously necessary just as more tinkering is needed to develop courts and galleries that will accommodate bigger crowds for squash tournaments. The Wembley Court in London where the British Open is now played has a glass back and can seat two hundred and fifty spectators for a top match. But what's clearly needed is a court with glass on three sides that'll give many more fans a view of the action. Already a manufacturer in

England is working on a portable court along those lines, and when that's perfected, and when TV and tournament sponsors get into the act in a big way, squash will really take off.

As for the professional circuit, it's been shaping up these last few years in grand style. At least, it has for the men. The top male soft-ball players can now keep on the move from tournament to tournament, from England to South Africa to Australia, for over six months of the year. And the best of them can win good money for their efforts. Geoff Hunt of Australia, the number one man in squash, won seventeen of twenty-two tournaments in 1976 and earned $40,000 exclusive of all his revenue from exhibitions and endorsements.

I wish the picture were as rosy in women's professional squash. It isn't. When I won the first-ever Women's World Championship at Brisbane in 1976, I received $2,000 in prize money. That amounted to exactly $1,500 more than I had ever received as a winner's share in any previous tournament. Women's squash, so far anyway, doesn't reward its champions more than meagerly. When the British Championship turned into an open tournament in 1974, allowing professionals to compete for the first time, its first prize was only fifty pounds, raised to one hundred pounds in 1977. Obviously what we need in women's squash are more sponsors like Australia's Queensland Permanent Building Society, which put up $6,000 for the first Women's World Championship, and like Bancroft, the American sporting equipment company that financed the hard-ball tournament in New York in 1977, paying $2,000 as first prize. Obviously we need sponsors, and just as obviously we need a women's squash circuit, a consistent series of professional tournaments rather than the bits and pieces system that's now the order of the day.

Call me a dreamer, but I think that we women pros will eventually realize both a tournament series and a respectable scale of prize money. The big question — when? — is the crucial matter for me. I turned thirty-six years old on July 31, 1977, and it might be hard to predict how long I can keep myself fit and able to win tournaments. On the non-competitive side of squash, Brian and I have no complaints at all. We're co-professionals at the Toronto Squash Club, and both of us find teaching squash a rewarding way to make a living from every standpoint.

It's the competitive part of my career, the part that got me where I am today, that raises the questions. Is thirty-six old? Not necessarily, as squash players go. Look at the great Hashim Khan who has continued through his forties, fifties and sixties beating men more than half his age. And besides I don't *feel* old. My game hasn't deteriorated, and whatever I've lost, if anything, in my original non-stop hitting-and-running style, I've more than compensated for in experience. I'm a smarter player than I used to be, and if you check the record, you'll see that I'm still beating my opponents and still winning all the tournaments I enter. The only part of the game that's become a grind is the training. When I think of the grueling three-month program that Brian put me through in preparation for the Women's World Championship, I want to scream. So does my body. And I wonder whether I could ever again endure that sort of extended regimen. On second thought, that isn't entirely accurate; I could put myself on the old training tomorrow or next year or maybe even in 1980 if a sponsor suddenly announced that he had $30,000 to invest in a women's squash tournament. For that, I could probably endure anything.

But even after I've given up active competition, I still expect to make my presence felt in squash in at least one way. I'll still be carrying on, mostly through teaching and coaching, what I learned long ago from people like Jean and Keith Walker and Vincent Napier and Janet Morgan about the special spirit of squash. I'll try to keep it alive because it's unique — and who knows that better than I do?

Jack Batten, the author of nine books, practiced law for several years before moving to journalism in the mid sixties. He is a regular contributor to several North American magazines on topics ranging from politics to sports. His book, The Leafs of Autumn, was a Book-of-the-Month Club alternate selection in November 1975. His most recent book was The Complete Jogger.